The American Bed & Breakfast Cookbook

The Bed Post Writers Group

The East Woods Press
Charlotte, North Carolina
Boston   ·   New York

Library of Congress Cataloging in Publication Data
Main entry under title:

The American bed & breakfast cookbook.

    Includes indexes.
    1. Breakfasts.   2. Brunches.   I. Bed Post Writers
Group.   II. Title: American bed and breakfast cookbook.
TX733.A44   1985   641.5'2   84-48886
ISBN 0-88742-052-4

Cover photograph by Robert Grubbe.
Illustrations by Diane Scott-Lombardo.
Typography by Carolina Compositors, Charlotte.
Printed in the United States of America.

Published by The East Woods Press
Fast & McMillan Publishers, Inc.
429 East Boulevard
Charlotte, NC 28203
(704) 334-0897

With love and gratitude to:
Dan . . . Tom and Rurik . . . Harry, Gina and Gate . . .
Dan, Pete, Mike and Kim.

And our heartfelt thanks for that extra assist to:
Jackie Davies, Sheila Dusinberre, Cathy Winters and
Sylvia Bashline . . . plus all others who tested,
tasted and touted our B&B effort.

Contents

Preface

THE IDEA for *THE AMERICAN BED & BREAKFAST COOKBOOK* came to us—Sandra Barker, Sandra Fullerton, Joanne Goins and Carol Yarrow—in answer to the question, "Why not?" Why not do a cookbook dedicated to the perpetuation of the bed and breakfast concept of good home cooking away from home?

We are not without experience. All have enjoyed delicious breakfasts and brunches at bed and breakfast establishments. Two of us, Fullerton and Barker, are members of Bed & Breakfast of Philadelphia and have hosted travelers from the U.S., Europe and the far East. Yarrow and Goins have chaired many church/school gourmet food booths and attended several cooking schools. All of us have been professionally occupied: Barker in needlework, Fullerton in the graphic arts and insurance, Goins in public relations and advertising and Yarrow in catering and the restaurant field. Fullerton, Goins and Yarrow are also co-owners of The Bed & Breakfast of Philadelphia Reservation Service.

So we formed a partnership, The Bed Post Writers Group, and began our work: contacting bed and breakfast agencies all over the country, compiling lists, sending request letters to hundreds of bed and breakfast establishments, sorting through return mail and much more. And then, of course, came the testing, and sometimes retesting, of the hundreds of recipes we received. And finally, when we had culled down to the 200 wonderful recipes in the book, we had to set about finding a publisher.

It is our hope that you get the same satisfaction and pleasure from this no-nonsense cookbook that we did in putting it together and do now in using it!

Introduction

A FAMILY, headed somewhat apprehensively toward their first bed and breakfast experience, found itself caught in a mid-Western blizzard. When they finally arrived, they were greeted by a roaring fire, hot chocolate, complimentary wine and a host who had been equally concerned about their lateness.

This pleasing story exemplifies the essence of American bed and breakfast: down-home hospitality. It can take many forms . . . as in the story of the German visitor whose host took her to the neighborhood square dance and then arranged for a local historian to take her on tour of the area. You can imagine how much more meaningful this visit was than a guidebook-oriented, motel stay would have been!

Warmth and friendship come hand in hand with hospitality and are the inevitable results of America's enthusiastic adoption of this mode of travel. More and more travelers are turning to bed and breakfast, because, as one first-timer puts it, "It's hard sometimes to try something new, but once you do and have such a positive experience, a new world is opened to you."

The variety of bed and breakfast establishments is enormous, including cottages, horse farms, historic townhouses, city highrises, elegant manors and many others. Rates vary too, but are generally lower than those of conventional motels and hotels. Whatever the style or price, there is a lodging for almost everyone.

Variety, hospitality and creativity are most evident in the outstanding, and often lavish, breakfasts, brunches and snacks prepared for bed and breakfast guests. This cookbook is a collection of personal favorite recipes of bed and breakfast hosts from all over the country . . . quality American cooking that reflects regional and ethnic diversity and plain, homey goodness. Recipes range from light starters to hearty entrees with frequent suggestions about combining foods to create menus. Cooking directions retain the chatty anecdotes and helpful suggestions from the bed and breakfast hosts. Any cook will relish this one-of-its-kind cookbook which makes the morning meal an event to be savored and prolonged. Just as the bed and breakfast tradition will continue to grow, *THE AMERICAN BED & BREAKFAST COOKBOOK* provides enough goodness to span many, many years!

Tips for Hosts

HELPFUL hints are included throughout this cookbook. They are useful, simple tips to help make guesting easier. Garnered from hosts across the country, the ideas are applicable in anyone's home and are helpful in making any meal or "overnight" a delightful experience.

The following are some general tips for hosts. Other tips, when applicable for specific recipes, will appear with those recipes.

☐ Evening Welcomer: A carafe of wine with appropriate glasses and nibbles, such as peanuts or health mix, etc., provide needed refreshment.

☐ A wicker basket of fresh fruits and a plate of homemade cookies set the mood for the visit.

☐ Filling a candy dish with locally-made sweets, plus a specialty from the guests' part of the country, bind the ties.

☐ Guest Book: B&B'ers are asked to sign in. Many are delighted to see a friend's name, making them feel even more "at home."

☐ Supplying a guest key on an oversized key chain upon arrival and collected on departure, provides freedom for some.

☐ The Room: Never just a "room" in B&B guesting. Make it extra special by including interesting objects. Perhaps you have a book on the room's history to leave for bedside reading, or a clock salvaged from a railroad station by Grandfather. Paintings by artist friends, an antique wash basin and pitcher, a special anniversary gift and old lace bed pillows collected from travels are beginnings for great conversation.

☐ "Welcome to Heatherlea": Fresh-cut garden flowers with a card of "WEL-COME," stating, "We hope you enjoy this B&B experience. We are here to see to that! If we have overlooked anything, please let us know. Sleep well!
Signed _____ (host name)

P.S.: We will not force ourselves on you, nor invade your privacy, but, please feel free to join us in the swimming pool, hot tub or watching TV in the family room." [Provide a wipe-off laminated sheet, on which to present the breakfast menu, allowing the guest to choose a convenient time.]

☐ Needed but forgotten travel extras: Keep a supply of reserve toiletries (mouthwash, razors, toothbrushes, aftershave and cologne samples, etc.), shoe shining essentials and a sewing kit neatly, but obviously, placed on a bathroom shelf.

☐ Tuck an assortment of individually wrapped guest soaps into a large brandy snifter.

☐ Extra conveniences, such as disposable laundry bags, eye shades and airline-type slipper socks, are appreciated.

☐ Leave a bucket of ice and cocktail glasses for travelers bringing their own liquor case.

☐ The latest *New York Times* crossword puzzle book, and *Readers' Digest* condensed books, magazines, paperbacks, and, of course, *The American Bed & Breakfast Cookbook*, displayed in an antique cradle, make leisure moments pleasurable.

☐ Area reference materials such as brochures on local attractions, menus from restaurants of varying price scales with travel directions attached, area maps (easily obtainable from local real estate offices) and museum and theatre information are greatly appreciated. These, plus a list of the appropriate telephone numbers at your guests' disposal, are welcome time-savers.

☐ Offering a "picnic basket" lunch for guests and a map of local parks allows them to make the most of their days. Available in the basket, along with the edibles, are dishes, tablecloth, napkins, utensils, salt and pepper, Thermos and, of course, a wine opener. A standard picnic lunch menu could be croissants stuffed with various salads, a Thermos of iced soup, seasonal fruit, layer cake, sodas and chilled wine.

☐ To conserve space on an umbrella table, fill a ring mold with fresh flowers and put the umbrella pole through the center.

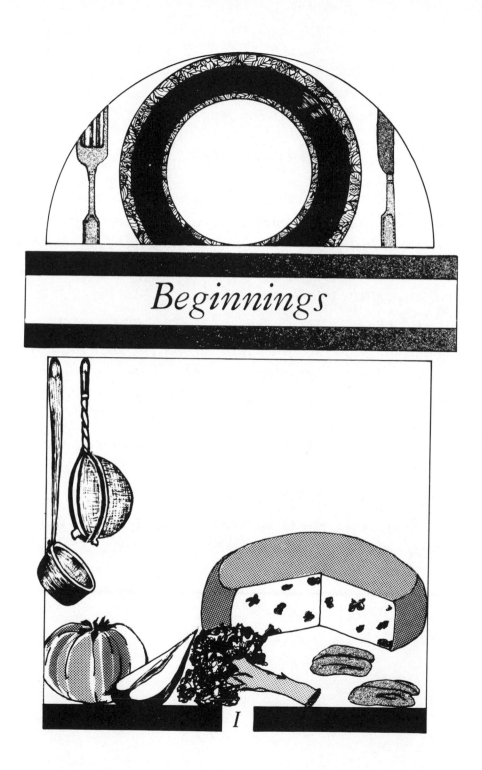

Beginnings

I

Beginnings

THAT "first impression!" You always want to make it a good one, as it's the "beginning" of any friendship or partnership. When guests come to your breakfast table you'll want a good beginning, well-knowing that the first glimpse and taste set the tone for what follows.

B&B hosts boast their breakfast "beginnings!" They enjoy entertaining for breakfast, turning the first meal of the day into a gala breakfast party. This chapter accommodates the host who has either few or many guests to serve, with beverages—hot, cold, alcoholic or not; soups for all seasons—interchangeable as mainstays for dinner or lunch; and fruits and toppings—mixing at cocktail parties, afternoon teas, brunches and luncheons.

These recipes are true "starters," but don't stop here. This is only the beginning.

BEVERAGES

Many a "good morning" starts with the first sip of hot coffee or a steaming mug of tea. Whether it is the morning rush, a relaxed repast or a gala breakfast party, with few or many guests to serve, you'll want a variety of beverages.

Freshly squeezed grapefruit from backyard trees and kitchen-ground coffees may be companions to the zingy zests of a hotly laced "Bloody."

To cold libations add a twist of citrus rind and serve in frosted stemware for a festive touch. To frost a glass (before filling) swab the rim with a lemon section or grenadine, swirl to remove excess liquid, and dip in granulated sugar. Lift glass and tap gently to remove excess sugar.

Make-ahead freezer treats and homemade mixes allow guests soothing comforts for any hour of the day, with a robust beverage taken "neat" from a mug. Enjoy the following beverages to "perk up" or "gear down," but don't stop here. This is only the first "beginning."

Apple Cider (Hot Mulled)

1 quart apple cider
8 whole cloves
2/3 cup brown sugar
1/4 teaspoon nutmeg
1 stick cinnamon
1/4 teaspoon ginger
Thin lemon slices for garnish

Combine cider, cloves, sugar, nutmeg, cinnamon and ginger in a 2-quart saucepan. Simmer 5 minutes. Pour into individual mugs or heatproof glasses; garnish with lemon. Yield: 6 servings.

Delores Skoglund
"SKOGLUND FARM," SOUTH DAKOTA

■ For the sweet smells of Christmas, keep a pot of this simmering on the back burner. It fills the house with a wonderful aroma and is ready when those cold skiers and tree choppers stomp in.

Big Banana Frappe

1 can (46 ounces) pineapple juice
1 can (46 ounces) orange juice
4 cups sugar
8 cups water*
5 cups mashed banana
1/2 cup lemon juice

In large mixing bowl, combine juices, sugar, water and banana, stirring until well blended. Turn into quart freezer containers, then freeze† Thaw approximately 30 minutes before serving "slushy." Yield: 6 quarts or 25 1-cup servings.

*Conserve freezer space by making a concentrate—add water at serving time instead of before freezing. Pack in 1-quart containers and use within 3 months. Yield: 4 quarts concentrate.

†Quarts freeze solid overnight.

Linda Johnson
OZARK MOUNTAIN COUNTRY
BED & BREAKFAST SERVICE, MISSOURI

Cantaloupe Crush

1 ripe cantaloupe, peeled and seeded
8 ounces plain yogurt
1 teaspoon vanilla extract
1/4 cup orange juice
Fresh mint sprigs for garnish

Cut cantaloupe into cubes. Place cubes in blender with yogurt, vanilla and juice. Puree 2 minutes or until liquified. Serve in tall glasses with straws for sipping and a sprig of mint for garnish. Yield: 2 servings.

The riper the cantaloupe, the better.

Sandra Fullerton, Host
BED & BREAKFAST OF
PHILADELPHIA, PENNSYLVANIA

Herbed Bloody Mary

6 ounces vegetable juice cocktail
2 ounces vodka
1 teaspoon herb vinegar (basil, tarragon or dill)
Dash Worcestershire sauce
Freshly ground black pepper
Lemon slice

Combine vegetable juice, vodka, vinegar and Worcestershire. Stir and pour into glass over ice. Sprinkle with a grind of black pepper and garnish with lemon slice. Yield: 1 serving.

"The Garrett-Drake House"
SOUTHERN COMFORT BED & BREAKFAST
RESERVATION SERVICE, LOUISIANA

Los Gatos Sunshine Riser

■ To serve guests a long-stemmed wine goblet filled with a tantalizing iced drink in bed, on wake-up call, is luxury, and is done by a Los Gatos, California, host . . .

1 can (6 ounces) frozen orange juice
1 cup water
4 ice cubes
1 cup vanilla ice cream
Water (optional)

Blend juice, water, ice cubes and ice cream in blender. Add water if too thick. Serve in two long-stemmed wine goblets. Serve guests while still in bed. Yield: 3 servings (one for the cook!)

HOME SUITE HOMES, SUNNYVALE, CALIFORNIA

Orange Eggnog

"This was my mother's 'cure' for anything. It also serves well as a quick, complete breakfast. For someone on the run, serve with a bran muffin, and you will have a filling, nutritious breakfast."

    1 egg, separated
    8 ounces orange juice
    1 tablespoon honey
    1 tablespoon wheat germ

In blender, combine egg yolk, orange juice, honey and wheat germ; whip 1 minute. In a separate bowl, beat egg white until stiff. Pour orange juice mixture into a large glass; top with beaten egg white. Yield: 1 serving.

Sandra Fullerton, Host
BED & BREAKFAST OF
PHILADELPHIA, PENNSYLVANIA

Ozark Mountain Buttered Rum Mix

The quickest of beverages are those from a ready-made mix. With its five variations, the Johnson household's Buttered Rum mix will help you charm any guest.

    6 cups brown sugar, firmly packed
    1 cup butter or margarine, melted
    3 tablespoons honey
    1 tablespoon vanilla extract
    1 tablespoon rum extract
    1 tablespoon brandy extract
    1 teaspoon ground cinnamon
    1/4 teaspoon ground nutmeg

In large mixing bowl, combine sugar, butter, honey, vanilla, rum and brandy extracts, cinnamon and nutmeg. Beat with electric mixer until well blended. Store in covered container in refrigerator up to three months. Yield: about 6 cups mix or 24 mug-size portions. To serve, place 1 teaspoon mix into each mug, and add one of the following:

    6 ounces hot apple or orange juice, or
    6 ounces hot milk, or
    6 ounces hot coffee with cream, or
    6 ounces boiling water with a jigger of rum

Stir to combine, using a peppermint stick as a swizzle.

Linda Johnson
OZARK MOUNTAIN COUNTRY
BED & BREAKFAST SERVICE, MISSOURI

Perk-Up Tea

1 cup powdered fruit juice mix
1 cup sugar
1/2 cup instant tea
1 tablespoon cinnamon
1/2 tablespoon ground cloves
1/2 tablespoon allspice
1 tablespoon grated lemon rind

Mix all ingredients together and store in tight container to have on hand for instant hot beverage.

To use, stir 2 teaspoons of mix into 1 cup of boiling water. Yield: 50 cups.

"Gloria often serves this to her B&B'ers when they return from trekking around historic German Village where she lives."

Gloria Soderholm, Host
COLUMBUS BED & BREAKFAST, OHIO

Sparkling Summer Punch

This punch has zing, even though it's non-alcoholic.

25 fresh mint leaves*
3/4 cup sugar
2 cups boiling water
1 can (6 ounces) frozen limeade concentrate (undiluted)
1 quart white grape juice, chilled
2 cups tonic water, chilled
1½ quarts lemon/lime soda, chilled
1 quart ginger ale, chilled
1 small sprig fresh mint per serving (optional)
Lime slices (optional)
Maraschino cherries (optional)

Crush the 25 mint leaves. Add to boiling water, along with sugar. Simmer for 15 minutes. Allow to cool; strain. This mint base may be refrigerated for several weeks. Yield: About 2 cups.

When ready to serve, mix mint base with limeade, grape juice, tonic, lemon/-lime soda and ginger ale. Pour into punch bowl. Yield: 4 to 5 quarts, or about 25 servings. This recipe doubles nicely.

Colorful garnishes could be an attractive ice mold in center of punch bowl and a lime slice with maraschino cherry on a swizzle stick, sharing the limelight with a sprig of mint in each punch cup.

Joan Brownhill
PINEAPPLE HOSPITALITY, INC.
BED & BREAKFAST, MASSACHUSETTS

■ *When fresh mint is unavailable, steep 6 mint tea bags in 2 cups boiling water. Add sugar and proceed with this recipe.
This punch is a great mixer for gin or vodka, also.

The Vermonter

Here's one for the kids. With a shot of your favorite brandy added, it warms adult tummies after a cold run on the trail.

>3/4 cup ice cold milk
>2 tablespoons maple syrup
>Small scoop vanilla ice cream

Blend milk with syrup and ice cream or shake the old-fashioned ice cream parlour way. Yield: 1 serving.

Linda Precoda
AMERICAN BED & BREAKFAST, VERMONT

SOUPS

Imagine the surprise of breakfast guests as you serve soup as their premiere to the day! Travelers ponder how they ever could have lived without it, while later in the day the family enjoys soup as a meal-in-itself.

Whether it's a simple gathering with few or many guests to serve, there are soups for all seasons. Advance preparation allows cooks to interchange these recipes. Soup is also a delectable way to warm up (or cool down) any weekend brunch.

Amish Tomato-Noodle Soup

"Amish simplicity is very tasty. Neighboring with many old Order Amish, we've learned to live simply, as they do, baking our own breads, raising vegetables and herbs—which we serve. The Amish provide us with the poultry, meat and egg products needed. I think the secret to Amish cooking is their flavoring of all foods with lots of butter, and their adjusting of flavors as they cook."

>1 quart home canned tomatoes, or 1 can (28 ounces) crushed tomatoes
>16 ounces water
>1/2 cup butter
>1 package (8 ounces) thin egg noodles
>1 quart milk
>1 pint cream or half-and-half
>Salt to taste
>Sugar to taste

In large soup kettle, bring tomatoes and water to a boil. Add butter and noodles, simmering until noodles are tender, 10 to 12 minutes, stirring occasionally to prevent sticking. Stir in milk, cream and seasonings. Heat, but do NOT boil. Yield: About 4 quarts or 16 first-course servings.

Burretta Redhead
"MASON HOUSE INN," IOWA

Beer-Cheese Soup

Most good cooks value cheese as a meat substitute. In Colonial New England, this soup was often a supper dish, with ale or beer the replacement for stock, and the cheese (Yankee Cheddar, Plymouth or Colby) cut from the provision store wheel. Today, it's equally at home, when served on a Northern ski slope or in a sunny Florida room.

  4 cups water
  4 chicken bouillon cubes
  1/2 cup butter
  1 cup flour
  1 quart half-and-half
  1 pound cheddar cheese, shredded
  1 can (12 ounces) beer
  Bacon bits

Bring water to boil in a large kettle. Dissolve bouillon cubes in water; set aside. Melt butter in large saucepan. Gradually stir in flour, eliminating lumps. Slowly add half-and-half, stirring until smooth.

Place kettle of bouillon over medium heat. Gradually add flour and milk mixture, stirring constantly. Blend in cheese and stir until melted. Slowly pour in beer. Heat thoroughly—do NOT boil. Serve piping hot, topped with bacon bits. Yield: 12 cups or 14 first-course servings.

Danie Bernard, Host
SUNCOAST ACCOMMODATIONS, FLORIDA

■ Spice to taste with salt, pepper and Worcestershire sauce. Sprinkle with chopped egg, paprika or Chili Nuts (page 162). Also, serve with rusks.

Blueberry-Raspberry Soup

4 cups water
6 tablespoons quick-cooking tapioca
1 cup sugar
1/2 teaspoon salt
4 sticks cinnamon, each 1½" long
2 teaspoons grated lemon peel
2/3 cup lemon juice
3 cups blueberries
4 packages (10 ounces each) frozen raspberries
Sour cream for garnish

In a 2-quart saucepan combine water, tapioca, sugar, salt, cinnamon, lemon peel, lemon juice and blueberries. Bring mixture to a boil over medium-high heat, stirring constantly. Reduce heat and simmer for 5 minutes, stirring occasionally.

Remove from heat and stir in raspberries and their liquid until blended. Cover and refrigerate at least 2 hours. Top with a dollop of sour cream to serve. Yield: 12 servings.

Nan Hawkins
BARNARD-GOOD HOUSE of CAPE MAY, NEW JERSEY

Colonial Peanut Soup

2 tablespoons minced onion
1/2 cup thinly sliced celery
2 tablespoons butter
2 tablespoons flour
4 cups chicken broth
1/3 cup creamy peanut butter
1/4 teaspoon salt
2 tablespoons lemon juice
2 tablespoons dry sherry
2 tablespoons chopped roasted peanuts

In large skillet, saute onion and celery in butter until onion is transparent, about 3 minutes. Gradually blend in flour. Add chicken broth, stir and simmer 15 to 20 minutes. Remove from heat. Strain and set aside.

Combine peanut butter, a little at a time, with broth mixture in large pan, stirring until smooth. Heat thoroughly, adding salt, lemon juice and sherry just before serving. Serve hot, garnished with chopped peanuts. Yield: 6 cups or 8 first-course servings.

When reheating, achieve desired consistency by adding more chicken broth.

Paula Gris, Madalyne Eplan and Jane Carney
BED & BREAKFAST ATLANTA, GEORGIA

Cream of Almond Soup

1½ cup blanched almonds
6 large leeks, trimmed, washed, cut into 4" pieces
3 medium size celery ribs
4½ tablespoons butter
6 cups homemade chicken broth
Salt to taste
1/4 teaspoon white pepper
1/4 to 1/2 teaspoon ground mace
3 cups light cream
Snipped fresh parsley or chives

In food processor buzz almonds until fine crumbs; set aside. With slicing disk, thinly slice celery and leeks. Melt butter in large heavy pan and saute just until leeks and celery are golden, 4 to 5 minutes. Add the almonds, chicken broth and spices. Cover and simmer 40 to 45 minutes, stirring occasionally.

Remove from heat and cool to room temperature. Strain. Put solids in processor with metal blade and buzz until pureed smooth. Combine with strained out liquid and cream. Reheat to serve, or serve chilled. Garnish with parsley or chives. Yield: 12 servings.

Nan Hawkins
BARNARD-GOOD HOUSE of CAPE MAY, NEW JERSEY

Cream of Carrot Soup

2 cups washed, peeled and sliced carrots
1 large onion, thinly sliced
1 clove garlic, minced
2 tablespoons uncooked rice
1 tablespoon minced parsley
Grated rind of 1/2 orange (reserve juice)
4 cups chicken stock
Juice of 1/2 orange (above)
Salt and pepper to taste

Combine carrots, onion, garlic, rice, parsley, orange rind and stock in soup kettle. Bring to boil, lower heat and simmer until carrots are tender, about 15 minutes. Allow soup to cool. Pour into blender, blending until smooth. Strain through fine sieve and return to kettle. Stir in orange juice, salt and pepper to taste. Heat to desired serving temperature. Yield: 6 cups or 8 first-course servings.

Gayle Garrison, Host
HOME SUITE HOMES, CALIFORNIA

■ Serve topped with a dollop of sour cream, and a sprinkling of fresh dill or grated nutmeg. As with most soups, this one is even better reheated, after an overnight in the refrigerator.

Daisy's Crab Bisque

"Daisy Redman—Toast of Savannah—was one of Savannah's best caterers. Daisy used our home for many of her catered functions, such as weddings or Historical Society gatherings. Our guests loved her. Daisy died last January, leaving me this recipe, one of her favorites."

1 pound backfin lump crabmeat
1 cup butter
2½ tablespoons flour
1 lemon, sliced
4 cups light cream
1/2 cup cream sherry
1 teaspoon salt
1/4 teaspoon white pepper
Tabasco to taste
Paprika

Pick over crabmeat, removing any shell or cartilage; set aside. In large heavy saucepan, over low heat, melt butter. With wooden spoon stir in flour until thoroughly blended. Add lemon and cream. Stir until smooth, and mixture comes to a boil. Immediately lower heat and simmer about 5 minutes. Fold in sherry, crabmeat, salt, pepper and Tabasco. Sprinkle each serving with paprika. "I always serve my soups in heated individual bowls." Yield: 6 to 8 servings.

Barbara Hershey for Daisy
"Stoddard Cooper House"
BED & BREAKFAST SAVANNAH, GEORGIA

Lost Bowl Farm Chicken Soup

Soup:
3½ pounds stewing chicken, cut up
5 cups water
2 teaspoons salt
1/4 teaspoon pepper
1/4 teaspoon dried basil leaves
1 bay leaf
Noodle dough:
1¼ cups flour
1 teaspoon salt
1 egg
1 cup creamed corn, crushed

Place chicken in large kettle, cover with 5 cups water, salt, pepper, basil and bay leaf. Simmer, covered, for 1½ hours or until chicken is tender.

While chicken is cooking, make noodle dough by mixing flour, salt and egg thoroughly with a spoon or hands. Let rest for awhile for easier handling.

When chicken is done, remove it from pot and let cool enough to handle. Discard bay leaf and skim fat from stock. Bring stock to boil and form noodle dough into rivulets by crumbling between palms and letting it fall randomly into pot. Boil for 3 to 4 minutes.

Bone and skin cooked chicken and cut into bite-size pieces. Add chicken and crushed creamed corn to pot and heat through. "Serve and accept compliments graciously." Yield: 4 to 6 servings.

"Lost Bowl Farm"
BETSY ROSS B&B, MICHIGAN

■ Chopped carrots, celery with leaves and onion may be added to pot with stewing chicken for richer stock. Throw in a sprig of fresh dill at end of simmer time.

Iced Cucumber Soup

1 medium onion, chopped
1 tablespoon butter
2 medium cucumbers, peeled, seeded
3 cups chicken stock
1/2 cup sour cream
Salt and white pepper to taste
1/4 cup minced green onion for garnish

Saute onion in butter until tender, about 3 minutes. Add cucumbers, coarsely chopped; cook about 3 minutes, stirring. Add chicken stock; simmer 15 minutes. Puree in blender, 1 cup at a time. Refrigerate several hours or overnight.

Just before serving, stir some of the soup into the sour cream until it is smooth and flowing. Combine with remaining soup, salt and pepper. Pour into chilled bowls and garnish with green onions. Yield: 8 servings.

Lillian Marshall
KENTUCKY HOMES B&B, KENTUCKY

■ Lil's "Good Morning" = Equal parts orange juice and beef bouillon, well chilled. "Good Night" = 2 liqueur glasses on a little silver tray with a bottle of something really marvelous, such as Frangelico liqueur, Kahlua, etc., placed on bedside table while guests are out for the evening.

Mushroom Chowder

Paul and Judy have a "two-for-one" for you. They easily convert this recipe to barley-mushroom chowder by omitting the potatoes and cooking a half-cup barley in the stock for 30 minutes, then proceeding with the recipe.

1/4 pound butter
1 cup chopped onion
4 cups boiling chicken broth or beef stock
1 cup sliced celery
1 cup diced carrots
1 pound mushrooms, washed and sliced
1 cup diced potatoes
3 medium tomatoes, skinned, seeded and chopped
1 teaspoon crushed thyme or oregano
2 tablespoons minced parsley
Salt and pepper to taste

In large Dutch oven, melt butter and saute onion until tender. Add broth and bring to boil. Stir in celery, carrots, mushrooms, potatoes and tomatoes. Simmer, covered, for 15 minutes. Add thyme or oregano and parsley. Season to taste with salt and pepper. Serve hot, topped with herbed or garlic croutons for crunch. Yield: 6 cups or 8 first-course servings.

Paul and Judy Barker
LOCH LYME LODGE AND COTTAGES, NEW HAMPSHIRE

■ For stronger flavor, simmer 2 hours and add 1/2 teaspoon minced chervil, 2 cloves minced garlic and 1/4 cup dry sherry the last hour.

Fruit Soup

4 cups prunes, pitted and chopped
2 cups citrus fruits (oranges, lemons, limes) unpeeled, sliced thin
2 cups blueberries
2 cups cherries, pitted
2 cups strawberries, hulled
4 cinnamon sticks
Water

Combine prunes, citrus, blueberries, cherries, strawberries and cinnamon in a large kettle. Cover with water. Bring to a boil, reduce heat and simmer for 2 hours. Remove cinnamon sticks and rinds from citrus fruits. Serve warm or chilled. Yield: 6 or more servings. "Good for brunch as a first course."

Pam Edson, Host
BETSY ROSS B&B, MICHIGAN

■ Rinse and spread blueberries on paper towel-covered cookie sheet. Blot with another paper towel to remove all moisture before freezing.

FRUIT AND TOPPINGS

Guests welcome a change to the traditional morning glass of juice, and B&B hosts thoughtfully start travelers on their way with these healthful starters. The following fruit and toppings can be the basis of any breakfast meal or contribute to the dinner repast.

Fruit is convenient, nutritional and pleasing to the eye, when heaped in a crystal compote, served simply as June strawberries dusted with powdered sugar or as July raspberries a la mode. A sprinkling of granola adds an interesting crunch also.

Toppings of yogurt, sour cream, whipped cream and liqueurs add light and tasty finishing touches to an ordinary fruit salad, making it elegant—effortlessly. Pancakes, waffles or pound cake can provide enjoyment throughout the day when crowned with special syrups and sauces.

"House honors" will be yours at any meal as you present the following creations to guests and family!

Aloha Salad Dressing

The memories return. An "aloha breakfast" on the lanai—an evening picnic on moonlit Hawaiian black sands. Serve your salads with this native salad dressing from Kauai.

> 1/2 cup sugar
> 1 teaspoon salt
> 1½ teaspoons dry mustard
> 1 cup red wine vinegar
> 2 cups vegetable oil
> 1/2 small onion, grated
> 2 tablespoons papaya seeds*
> 1/2 cup chopped macadamia nuts

Place sugar, salt, mustard and vinegar in blender and process until well combined. With machine on, gradually add oil until blended. Remove to large bowl; set aside.

In blender combine onion, papaya seeds and macadamia nuts. Process until finely ground. Fold the seed and nut mixture into mixture in bowl; combine well. Refrigerate until ready to use. Yield: 3½ cups.

Evie Warner
BED & BREAKFAST, HAWAII

■ *Papaya seeds from the fresh fruit may be used after drying, or you can substitute poppy seeds.
Excellent on chunky chicken or tuna salad. Tangy on fruit salad, as well as spinach and avocado/grapefruit salad, mixed veggies and tossed greens.

Bavarian Quark

"Last spring in Bavaria, I visited a lovely bed and breakfast home. One of the special delicacies I was served was 'Quark.' I have searched, but to my knowledge, its American counterpart is unobtainable. So, I have concocted a satisfactory substitute for use over stewed prunes and other fruit. We love it as a topping for hot old-fashioned scones and jam, too."

> 2 cups plain yogurt
> 1/2 cup sour cream
> Vanilla sugar* to taste
> Cinnamon

Place yogurt, sour cream and sugar in blender, blending until well combined. Chill thoroughly. Serve over sliced fresh fruit and sprinkle with cinnamon. Yield: About 2½ cups.

Elaine Silverman, Host
HOME SUITE HOMES, CALIFORNIA

■ *Make your own vanilla sugar by placing one vanilla bean in an airtight container with granulated sugar for approximately two weeks, or combine vanilla extract and granulated sugar.

■ During the testing of these recipes, Frau Eyde and daughter Verena from Hamburg, Germany, came to stay as B&B guests in our country. We were discussing "Quark" (which seems to be almost a German national dish) and before we knew it, we were in the kitchen experimenting, and concocted the following . . .

Using Ricotta cheese or heavy whipping cream as the base, mix with vanilla yogurt, a little lemon juice and small amount of sugar (to your taste). Blend with electric mixer until smooth. Layer fresh fruit (berries, melon, bananas, etc.) and "Quark" in stemmed sherbet glasses.

Another way of serving "Quark" is to mix in herbs and/or minced fresh vegetables (radishes, carrots, celery, etc.) and spread on Swedish hard crackers.

Frau Constance Eyde, Guest
Hamburg, Germany
Sandra Barker, Host
BED & BREAKFAST PHILADELPHIA, PENNSYLVANIA

Loch Lyme Delight

8 ounces plain yogurt*
2 tablespoons brown sugar or honey
1 teaspoon vanilla extract†
Mixed fruit bowl (recipe below)
Cinnamon

In small bowl, stir to combine yogurt, brown sugar or honey and vanilla. Place fruit from mixed fruit bowl or fresh strawberries in chilled parfait glasses. Top fruit with yogurt mixture and dust with cinnamon. Yield: About 1 cup topping.

*Use lemon yogurt and serve over pound cake.
†Substitute almond or coconut extracts or liqueurs.

Paul and Judy Barker
LOCH LYME LODGE AND COTTAGES, NEW HAMPSHIRE

Mixed Fruit Bowl

Pearl's perpetual fruit bowl begins with as many fresh or frozen fruits as are available—apples, bananas, peaches, cherries, pineapple, etc. Add canned fruit for sweetness. For variety, she adds orange juice concentrate, coconut and almonds. Keep this fruit bowl "on-going" in the refrigerator, adding fruits as they ripen. Top with Loch Lyme Delight when serving.

Pearl 'n' Rod Thurlow
BED 'N' BREAKFAST ON OUR FARM, KANSAS

Orange and Peach Salad

1 package (3 ounces) orange-flavored gelatin
1 cup hot water
1/4 cup orange juice
1/4 cup peach juice (reserved from peach halves)
1/2 cup ginger ale
1 can (1 pound, 2 ounces) peach halves
Maraschino cherries
1/2 cup pecan halves

Dissolve gelatin in hot water. Add orange juice, peach juice and ginger ale. Stir and refrigerate until "soupy" stage, about one-half hour. With pit or stone side up, place peach halves into a 1-quart serving bowl or place one peach half into each dessert dish.

Place one maraschino cherry in each peach half. Spoon gelatin mixture around peaches and over top. Place pecan halves on top of gelatin, alternately between peach halves. Return salad to refrigerator for several hours, until congealed. Yield: 6 to 8 servings.

Dorothy Bush, Host
New Orleans Bed & Breakfast, Louisiana

■ Delicious topped with Bavarian Quark (page 27).

Orange Lotus Cups

6 large navel oranges
1½ cups pitted cherries
1 can (13½ ounces) pineapple chunks
1½ cups apricot halves
1/3 cup margarine
1/4 cup brown sugar
1 teaspoon curry powder
Sour cream for garnish

To make orange cups, slice tops from oranges, cut around inside edges and remove fruit. Cut zigzag edge around tops of oranges.

Combine orange pulp with other fruits and divide into shells. Combine margarine, sugar and curry powder and place over tops of fruit-filled orange shells.

Wrap each cup in aluminum foil and bake in a 350° oven for 10 to 15 minutes. Top with a dollop of sour cream and serve immediately. Yield: 6 servings.

Dottie
Castle Keep Bed & Breakfast Registry, Rhode Island

Robert's Special Topping
and
Sunday Morning Fruit Salad

1 pint whipping cream
1 teaspoon freshly grated nutmeg
1 tablespoon vanilla extract
1¼ teaspoons grated orange peel
1/8 to 1/4 cup confectioners' sugar
1/4 cup orange liqueur
1 orange, halved
2 whole strawberries
Kiwi slices or pomegranate seeds
2 mint sprigs
Seasonal fresh fruit, cut up into bite-size pieces

Whip cream at high speed until thickened. Fold in vanilla, nutmeg, orange peel and sugar. Continue whipping until stiff peaks appear. Gently fold in orange liqueur.

Hollow each orange half; fill with topping. Place on serving platter and surround with fresh fruit. Garnish topping with strawberries, kiwi slices or pomegranate seeds and mint sprigs. Yield: About 2 cups topping.

Daun Martin
"BRITT HOUSE," CALIFORNIA

Texas Monterey Grapefruit

For the feeling of winter-time sunshine, I serve my guests fresh fruit, brewed coffee, and hot milk and honey over oatmeal!

1/2 English muffin
1 pink grapefruit slice, 1/4" thick, peeled
2 slices Monterey Jack cheese

Preheat broiler. Place muffin half on piece of aluminum foil. Top muffin with grapefruit slice and cheese. Place on sturdy oven-proof pan and broil until cheese melts. Yield: 1 serving.

Wilhelmina, Host
THE BED & BREAKFAST SOCIETY, TEXAS

Tootie Fruitie

For those other-than-mealtime arrivals, Kay's Tootie Fruitie can quickly fill the void. Within 10 minutes from the freezer, you can serve it to the children for a snack or to the adults for appreciated refreshment!

> 1 can (1 pound) fruit cocktail with liquid
> 3 bananas, peeled
> 1/2 cup shredded coconut or 2 tablespoons Pina Colada liqueur
> 12 lettuce leaves
> Mandarin orange sections (optional)
> Shredded coconut for garnish (optional)

In blender, combine fruit cocktail, bananas and coconut; process for 30 seconds to mix. Line 12 muffin cups with paper baking cup liners. Fill each muffin cup with mixture to 1/4 inch from top of paper. Freeze until firm.

Ten minutes before serving, remove from freezer and peel off paper. Do not allow to stand longer than 10 minutes. Place each over lettuce leaf, and garnish with mandarin orange sections and coconut, if desired. Yield: 12 servings.

Kay Cameron
OZARK MOUNTAIN COUNTRY
BED & BREAKFAST SERVICE, MISSOURI

■ Store in freezer bags or containers, after frozen, for up to 3 months in your freezer.

Yogurt Dressings

I

8 ounces plain yogurt
1/2 to 1 tablespoon prepared horseradish
1 tablespoon tarragon or garlic vinegar
1 tablespoon snipped chives
1 tablespoon dill weed
3/4 teaspoon salt
1/4 teaspoon paprika

In a medium-size bowl, stir together yogurt, horseradish, vinegar, chives, dill, salt and paprika. Cover and refrigerate for up to 3 days. Yield: 1 cup.

II

2 tablespoons lemon juice
1 tablespoon salad oil
1/2 cup plain yogurt
1/2 teaspoon paprika
Dash hot pepper sauce
1/2 teaspoon salt
Pinch garlic powder

Combine juice, oil, yogurt, paprika, pepper sauce, salt and garlic and refrigerate. Yield: 2/3 cup.

Norma Buzan
BETSY ROSS B&B, MICHIGAN

■ Both of these are lovely over spinach or tossed green salad. Serve with any of the great quiches and you have a satisfying breakfast, lunch or supper.

Arizona's Hawaiian Compote

1 can (20 ounces) unsweetened pineapple chunks and 1/2 of pineapple juice
3 bananas, peeled and sliced
2 papayas, sliced
1 package (7 ounces) shredded coconut

Gently combine pineapple and juice, bananas, papayas and coconut in a large bowl. Chill for 30 minutes and serve. Yield: About 1 quart.

Bessie Lipinski
BED AND BREAKFAST IN ARIZONA

■ Bessie serves this compote in an attractive shell or crystal-clear bowl. Colorful enough for a centerpiece when surrounded with hollowed pineapple halves filled with a variety of toppings.

Breads and Spreads

II

Breads, Muffins and Coffee Cakes

A TRIBUTE *to the grace of Bed and Breakfast prevails as guests awake to the aroma of freshly baked foodstuffs. This chapter presents a regional array of recipes from B&B hosts across the country. The number and variety of pet recipes are testimony to their place at the breakfast table.*

Breakfast breads—enjoyable throughout the day—can be made and frozen, if desired, and reheated at the last minute for ease and convenience. In this chapter, unless otherwise specified, recipes call for all-purpose flour, granulated sugar and a pre-heated oven.

If your supermarket does not stock the flours or gourmet ingredients, a health food store or specialty market probably will.

Standard loaf pan sizes, referred to in these recipes, are large (9-inch), medium (7-inch) and small and individual-size loaves (5-inch). With large loaves (called peasant, because of size) accurately slashing the top in a checkerboard pattern before baking will prevent a lopsided loaf. Also, try brushing some loaves with olive oil for a distinctive flavor.

Quick breads attract B&B hosts and any cook who wants to save time, yet bake a tasty loaf. Allow quick bread batter to sit at room temperature in the loaf pan for 15 to 20 minutes before baking for a lighter texture.

Many fruit and nut breads need a chance to season before eating. These loaves should not be sliced fresh and hot from the oven, but allowed to "set" a day. And, as with muffins, breads should be placed immediately on a rack to cool, when removed from the oven. These breads freeze well up to 3 months.

Several B&B hosts have a monthly "baking day." Customize your needs by choosing appropriate pan sizes. Cooled loaves should be wrapped tightly in aluminum foil or freezer paper (press all air from packages), labeled, dated and frozen. Keep a dated bread list on the freezer door for quick identification.

One host suggests keeping at least three different fruit breads on hand—each one distinct in flavor and texture. Serve them sliced and warm, or day-old and toasted, attractively lodged in an English toast holder and accompanied by several different spreads (Chapter 2). A basket filled with a variety of muffins is a quick, simple and nutritious way to greet the day.

B&B hosts are bountiful bakers, as evidenced by the volume and variety of breads, muffins, biscuits, sweet rolls and munchable coffee cakes in this chapter. Bed and Breakfast guests and family alike are the happy beneficiaries at the morning meal, brunch, tea or the midnight snack hour.

Almond Apricot Bread

1½ cups dried apricots
1/4 cup sugar
1 cup boiling water
2½ cups sifted all-purpose flour
4 teaspoons baking powder
1/2 teaspoon salt
1/2 cup chopped almonds
2 tablespoons butter
1/2 cup sugar*
1 egg
1 cup milk

Place apricots and 1/4 cup sugar in saucepan, and cover with 1 cup boiling water. Cook approximately 10 minutes, or let stand one hour.

While waiting for apricots to plump, grease and flour a 9" loaf pan. Sift flour, baking powder and salt together; set aside. Preheat oven to 350°.

Drain and chop apricots. Fold in almonds. In large mixing bowl, cream together butter, 1/2 cup sugar and egg. Beat well. Stir in fruit mixture. Add dry ingredients, alternately with milk, to batter, mixing well after each addition. Turn batter into prepared loaf pan. Bake one hour or until knife inserted into center comes out clean. Yield: 1 loaf.

*Use one cup sugar for sweeter bread. Sprinkle with confectioners' sugar before serving.

Olive Bree, Host
A REASONABLE ALTERNATIVE, INC., NEW YORK

■ Once peeled and sliced, fresh apricots will hold their color if dipped into an ascorbic acid mixture or lemon juice. The shelf life of packaged dried apricots is about 6 months.

Anise Orange Braid

1 cup milk, scalded
3/4 teaspoon salt
1/4 cup sugar
1/4 cup butter
1 package dry yeast
1/4 cup warm water
1 egg
1½ teaspoons grated orange peel
2 teaspoons anise seed, crushed
1/8 teaspoon mace
1/8 teaspoon nutmeg
3½ cups bread flour

Pour scalded milk over salt, sugar and butter in large bowl. Cool to luke-warm. Dissolve yeast in warm water. Add yeast, egg, orange peel, anise, mace and nutmeg to milk mixture, beating well. Stir in enough flour to make a soft dough. Turn out onto a floured board or pastry cloth and knead 10 minutes. Place in buttered bowl, cover with a kitchen towel and let rise until doubled in bulk, about 1 hour.

Punch down dough and divide into thirds.* Shape each third into a 15" rope, braid together, tucking under ends. Place braids in a greased 12" baking pan or dish. Cover and let rise to edge of pan, about 45 minutes.

Bake in a preheated oven at 350°, 35 to 40 minutes or until golden brown. Turn out on rack to cool. Yield: 1 large loaf.

Frost cooled loaf with icing made of confectioners' sugar and orange juice.

Pat Wells, Host
BED & BREAKFAST OF PHILADELPHIA, PENNSYLVANIA

■ *Twist into individual-sized guest braids for a personal touch. Freeze bread for later use, up to 3 months. Decorate top of braids with sliced gum drop candies, if you like.

Applesauce Oatmeal Bread

1½ cups pre-sifted all-purpose flour
1 teaspoon baking powder
1 teaspoon baking soda
1 teaspoon salt
1 teaspoon cinnamon
2/3 cup brown sugar
2 eggs
1 cup applesauce
1/4 cup melted butter
1½ cups quick rolled oats
1/2 cup chopped nuts

Preheat oven to 350°. In large mixing bowl, sift together flour, baking powder, soda, salt and cinnamon. Stir in brown sugar. Add eggs, applesauce and butter, beating well. Stir in oats and nuts and beat well. Turn into a greased and floured 9-inch loaf pan. Bake 1 hour. Yield: 1 loaf.

*Or use two 5-inch loaf pans and bake 45 minutes.

Barbara Fredholm
MID-MISSOURI BED AND
BREAKFAST SERVICE, MISSOURI

Beer Bread With Icing

Batter:
6 cups all-purpose flour
6 teaspoons baking powder
3 teaspoons salt
6 tablespoons sugar
2 cans (12 ounces each) beer

Icing:
1 cup butter
8 ounces cream cheese, softened
1 pound confectioners' sugar
1 teaspoon vanilla

Mix together flour, baking powder, salt, sugar and beer. Place in two greased 9- by 5-inch loaf pans. Start in a COLD oven. Bake at 375° for 60 to 70 minutes. When cool, top with icing.

To prepare icing, cream butter in a bowl with mixer and add cream cheese. Sift in confectioners' sugar. Add vanilla and beat until smooth. Spread over cooled bread. Yield: 2 loaves.

Marianne Schatz
THE ABBEY, NEW JERSEY

Bishop's Loaf

1 egg
1/3 cup water or maraschino cherry juice
2/3 cup mashed banana
1 box (1 pound) nut bread mix
1 package (8 ounces) chocolate chips
1 jar (10 ounces) maraschino cherries (reserve liquid, if using)

Preheat oven to 350°. Butter and flour a 2-pound coffee can or two 7-inch loaf pans. Combine egg, water or cherry juice, banana and nut mix in mixing bowl. Prepare according to package directions. Fold in chocolate chips and cherries.

Turn batter into prepared container. Bake approximately 55 minutes. Invert onto wire rack, and cool 10 minutes before removing from pan. If using Bundt pan, cool 10 minutes in upright position, then invert onto cooling rack. Yield: 1 large or 2 small loaves.

Bessie Lipinski
BED AND BREAKFAST IN ARIZONA

■ Add one cup finely chopped almonds or pecans for nuttier flavor, and sprinkle top— through lacey paper doily— with sifted confectioners' sugar, when hot out of oven.

Blueberry Nut Bread

2/3 cup shortening
1-1/3 cups sugar
4 eggs
1 cup milk
1½ teaspoons lemon juice
3 cups flour
2 teaspoons baking powder
1 teaspoon salt
1 teaspoon soda
1 cup crushed pineapple, drained
1 cup chopped nuts
2 cups fresh blueberries

Preheat oven to 350°. Cream together shortening and sugar. Beat in the eggs. Add milk and lemon juice, mixing well.

Sift together flour, baking powder, salt and soda; add to creamed mixture, a little at a time. Stir in crushed pineapple and nuts. Gently fold in blueberries.

Pour into three greased 7-inch loaf pans and bake for 45 minutes. Yield: 3 loaves.

June Bretl, Host
BED & BREAKFAST IN DOOR COUNTY, WISCONSIN

Charlotte's Deluxe Corn Bread

2 eggs
1 cup sour cream
1/2 cup vegetable oil
1 cup cream-style corn
1 cup cornmeal
1 to 1½ teaspoons salt, according to preference
3 teaspoons baking powder

Preheat oven to 375°. Beat eggs in large mixing bowl. Blend in sour cream, oil and corn. Sift dry ingredients together, and add to egg mixture, stirring until well combined. Pour into a greased 8″ square pan. Bake 30 to 45 minutes. Cool and cut into serving-size squares. Serves 6 to 8.

Charlotte Fairey
HISTORIC CHARLESTON BED
AND BREAKFAST, SOUTH CAROLINA

■ Betty Cordellos of Nashville Bed & Breakfast prefers a Mexican flavor. She adds one cup grated cheese, two tablespoons chopped onion and one 2-ounce can chopped chili peppers at the last minute and bakes per recipe.

Colonial Bread

■ "Colonial Bread" connotes stoneware mugs of coffee, freshly-churned sweet butter, thick bacon sizzling in an iron spider over an open fire in the "keeping room." Bring this romanticism to your B&B guests by serving delicious, individual loaves of bread, or rolls, neatly tucked into a Colonial kitchen cap of muslin or linen.

As Karen states, "One small loaf does very nicely for two people, breakfast or dinner. It is always gone when I clear the table."

2/3 cup yellow cornmeal
1/2 cup brown sugar, firmly packed
1 tablespoon salt
2 cups boiling water
1/4 cup solid vegetable shortening
2 packages dry yeast
1/2 cup very warm water (110 to 115° F.)
3/4 cup whole wheat flour
1/2 cup rye flour
4¼ to 4½ cups all-purpose flour or bread flour

Grease two 9-inch or five 3-inch loaf pans. Sprinkle each 9-inch pan bottom with 1 tablespoon cornmeal, and each 3-inch pan bottom with 1/2 tablespoon cornmeal.

In large bowl, thoroughly combine remaining cornmeal, brown sugar, salt, boiling water and shortening. Let cool to lukewarm, about 30 minutes.

Meanwhile soften yeast in 1/2 cup very warm water; then stir into cornmeal mixture. Add whole wheat and rye flours, mixing well. Work in enough white flour to make a moderately stiff dough.

Turn dough out onto a floured board and knead until smooth, 6 to 8 minutes. Return dough to greased bowl, cover, set in warm place to rise until double in bulk, 50 to 60 minutes.

Divide dough equally for number of pans used, let rest 5 minutes. Shape dough into prepared pans. Cover and let rise 30 to 40 minutes for large loaves, and 20 to 30 minutes for smaller ones. Preheat oven to 375° and bake* large loaves 45 minutes, and small loaves for 30 minutes. When bread pulls away from sides of pans, remove from oven and immediately turn out of pans. Yield: 2 large loaves or 5 small loaves.

*Brush dough with an egg and water glaze [1 egg white and 1 teaspoon water] before baking, for a golden bread.

Karen Gauntlett
"WELLMAN ACCOMMODATIONS," MICHIGAN

Date Nut Bread

1 cup water, boiling
1 cup sugar
1 teaspoon salt
1 teaspoon vanilla
1 tablespoon margarine
1 teaspoon baking soda
1/2 cup chopped pecans
1 cup finely chopped dates
1 egg, beaten
1½ cups all-purpose flour

In heat-proof bowl, pour boiling water over sugar, salt, vanilla, margarine, soda, pecans and dates. Mix well, and set aside to cool.

Grease and flour a 9-inch loaf pan. Preheat oven to 325°. Stir egg and flour into cooled mixture, until combined. Turn batter into prepared pan. Bake 1 hour. Yield: 1 loaf.

"A winner every time, when I serve with cream cheese."

Moselle Shaffer
"CAMEL LOT," INDIANA

Dorothy's Pear Bread

1/2 cup butter
1 cup sugar
2 eggs
2 cups all-purpose flour
1/2 teaspoon salt
1/2 teaspoon baking soda
1 teaspoon baking powder
1/8 teaspoon nutmeg
1/4 cup yogurt or buttermilk
2 medium pears, peeled, cored, chopped
1 teaspoon vanilla

Preheat oven to 350°. Grease a 9-inch loaf pan. Cream together butter and sugar in large mixing bowl. Beat in eggs, one at a time. Sift together flour, salt, baking soda, baking powder and nutmeg.

Add to creamed mixture, alternately with yogurt or buttermilk, mixing well after each addition. Fold in pears and vanilla. Turn into prepared pan and bake 1 hour, or until tester inserted in center of loaf comes out clean. Yield: 1 loaf.

Linda Rackard
BED & BREAKFAST OF CENTRAL NEW YORK

Easy Boston Brown Bread

2 cups raisins
2 tablespoons margarine
1 tablespoon baking soda
1 cup sugar
1½ cups boiling water
1 egg
2 cups all-purpose flour

Remove one end from each of four vegetable cans.* In bowl stir together raisins, margarine, baking soda and sugar. Cover with boiling water, stir and let stand overnight.

In morning, preheat oven to 350°. Grease inside of cans with vegetable cooking spray. Add the egg and flour to raisin mixture, stirring well. Divide batter evenly into each can. Bake, open end up, 50 minutes. Invert cans onto rack to cool. Slice bread into rounds and spread with cream cheese, strawberry cream cheese or your favorite spread. Yield: 4 to 6 servings.

*Or use two 1-pound coffee cans prepared the same way.

Norma Hannah, Host
"RANCHO BERNARDO"
HOME SUITE HOMES, CALIFORNIA

Gerda's Sourdough Wheat Bread

3/4 cup milk or 1/2 cup milk and 1/4 cup hot water
2 tablespoons butter or vegetable oil
1½ tablespoons honey
1 package dry yeast
3/4 cup sourdough starter (recipe follows)
3/4 cup whole wheat flour
1½ tablespoons wheat germ
2 teaspoons sugar
1 teaspoon salt
1/2 teaspoon baking soda
1½ cups unbleached flour

Preheat Crockpot for 30 minutes on high. In a small saucepan, scald milk. Add butter and honey to milk; allow to melt, then cool to lukewarm. Mix yeast in milk, stirring to dissolve.

Add sourdough starter, whole wheat flour and wheat germ. Blend sugar, salt and baking soda until smooth; sprinkle over top of dough, stirring gently.

Stir in unbleached flour until dough is too stiff to stir. Turn dough out onto a floured board, and knead 100 times. Shape into a loaf. Place in a well-greased 2-pound coffee can and cover with aluminum foil.

Place can in Crockpot. Cover pot and bake on high for 2 to 2½ hours, or until top is browned. Remove can and uncover. Let stand 5 minutes. Unmold onto a cake rack. Serve warm. Yield: 1 loaf.

Sourdough Starter

　　1 package dry yeast
　　2½ cups lukewarm water
　　2 cups flour
　　1 tablespoon sugar
　　1 teaspoon salt

In glass or crockery container, dissolve yeast in 1/2 cup lukewarm water. Add remaining ingredients. Mix well with a wooden or plastic spoon until smooth. Cover bowl with a towel and let stand at room temperature for 3 to 5 days, stirring several times EACH day. Then store covered in refrigerator. Add 1 teaspoon sugar, if not used within 10 days.

Gerda Carmichael, Host
BED & BREAKFAST BIRMINGHAM, INC., ALABAMA

German Tea Bread

"This recipe for 'Mama Bread,' as it is known in my family, was given to my maternal grandmother by her future mother-in-law as part of her wedding present. My grandmother would arrive for a visit looking fresh as a daisy after her 10-hour drive, with six loaves of this bread in the back seat beside jars of her spaghetti sauce."

1 cup milk
1½ cups butter or margarine
3/4 cup sugar
1 tablespoon salt, or to taste
1/2 cup warm water
1/2 teaspoon sugar
2 packages dry yeast
8 cups flour*
2 eggs, beaten

Scald milk and butter in saucepan, until butter is nearly melted. Cool partially. Add 3/4 cup sugar and 1 tablespoon salt. In small bowl, combine water and 1/2 teaspoon sugar. Add yeast; set aside.

Place 4 cups flour in large bowl; add milk mixture. Stir together. Add eggs and yeast mixture. Stir in 1/2 the remaining flour until smooth. Remove dough to a lightly greased bowl, turning once to grease dough while shaping into ball. Cover with towel, and allow to rise in warm place for 30 minutes or so.

Gradually stir in remaining flour. Add more flour if dough is too sticky. Knead until dough is smooth. Let rise again until double in bulk, about 1 hour. Punch down dough, cut into thirds, knead and shape. Place in three greased 9-inch loaf pans.† Preheat oven to 350°. Bake 15 minutes; reduce heat to 325° and bake an additional 15 minutes. Yield: 3 loaves.

*Whole wheat flour, or half whole wheat and half all-purpose may produce a texture more to your liking.
†Or use 7-inch loaf pans for higher rise.

Mary Fitzhugh
PIONEER VALLEY BED & BREAKFAST
NETWORK, MASSACHUSETTS

Herbed Corn Bread

1 package dry yeast
1/2 cup warm water
2 teaspoons celery seed
3 tablespoons sugar
1/8 teaspoon ginger
1/8 teaspoon marjoram
1 can (13 ounces) evaporated milk
2 tablespoons salad oil
1 teaspoon salt
1/2 cup yellow corn meal
3½ to 4 cups all-purpose flour, unsifted
Butter or margarine, softened

In large bowl, dissolve yeast in warm water. Blend in celery seed. Add 1 tablespoon sugar, the ginger and marjoram. Let stand until bubbly, about 15 minutes.

Stir in remaining 2 tablespoons of sugar, along with milk, oil and salt. Gradually beat in cornmeal and enough flour, 1 cup at a time, to make a very heavy, stiff batter, but too sticky to knead.

Divide batter in half, spoon into two well-greased 1-pound coffee cans (or one 2-pound can). Cover with cloth and stand in warm place until batter rises (50 minutes in small cans, 1 hour in large can). Bake, uncovered, in 350° oven for 45 minutes for small cans, 1 hour for large can. Brush tops with butter. Cool on rack for 10 minutes, remove from can and continue to cool. Yield: 2 small loaves or 1 large loaf.

Ellie Welch/Peg Tierney
BED & BREAKFAST REGISTRY, MAINE

Leone's Pineapple Zucchini Bread

3 eggs, beaten
1 cup oil
2 cups sugar
2 teaspoons vanilla
2 cups shredded zucchini
1 can (8¼ ounces) crushed pineapple, drained*
3 cups flour
1 teaspoon salt
2 teaspoons baking soda
1/2 teaspoon baking powder
1½ teaspoons cinnamon
3/4 teaspoon nutmeg
1 cup chopped walnuts
1 cup currants

Preheat oven to 350°. Beat eggs, oil, sugar and vanilla in large mixing bowl until foamy. Stir in zucchini and pineapple. Combine flour, salt, baking soda, baking powder, cinnamon, nutmeg, walnuts and currants. Gently stir into zucchini mixture. Bake in greased loaf pans, approximately 1 hour, slightly less for smaller loaves.

To accommodate seasonal needs, customize your baking. This recipe yields two 9-inch loaves, three 7-inch loaves or five 5-inch loaves. Tightly seal baked loaves in freezer wrap before freezing and you're ready.

Megan Backer
B 'N' B MEGAN'S FRIENDS, CALIFORNIA

■ *If you have the time and a fresh pineapple, use them. Judge a pineapple's ripeness by pulling an inner frond from the crown. If it pulls easily, the pineapple is ripe. To prepare, cut the pineapple in half, lengthwise, through the center, then cut each half lengthwise, making 4 quarters. Pare and remove the center core. Cube flesh and chop. Remove excess juice, if desired, by wringing cubed pineapple in dish towel.

No-Knead Whole Wheat Bread

"This is a stick-to-your-ribs bread, which substitutes for dinner rolls and goes with soup at lunchtime. We like it best sliced thick, with our morning eggs." Warming the flour cuts out the kneading and seems to be the secret in this recipe.

2 packages dry yeast
2/3 cup warm water
2 teaspoons honey

5 cups whole wheat flour
3 tablespoons molasses
2 tablespoons butter
1-1/3 cups warm water
1½ teaspoons salt
1/3 cup wheat germ
1/2 cup bran cereal
1/3 cup sesame seeds

Sprinkle yeast over 2/3 cup warm water, stir in honey and leave to work. Warm flour in 250° oven for 20 minutes. Combine molasses and butter with 2/3 cup water; mix with yeast mixture. Remove warm flour from oven. Stir liquid mixture into flour. Add salt, wheat germ, bran and remaining 2/3 cup water, mixing well. Dough will be sticky.

Divide dough into three greased 8-inch loaf pans. Sprinkle tops with sesame seeds, cover with towel, and let rise to top of pans. Bake in preheated 400° oven, 30 to 40 minutes. Yield: 3 loaves.

Evie Warner
BED & BREAKFAST HAWAII

Nutty Pumpkin Bread

3 cups sugar
1 cup shortening
4 eggs
1 can (16 ounces) pumpkin
2/3 cup water
3-1/3 cups all-purpose flour
1 teaspoon cinnamon
1 teaspoon nutmeg
1½ teaspoons salt
2 teaspoons baking soda
1 teaspoon vanilla
1 cup chopped nuts

Preheat oven to 350°. Grease three 7-inch loaf pans. Cream sugar and shortening together in large bowl. Add eggs, pumpkin and water, mixing well. Combine flour, cinnamon, nutmeg, salt and soda. Fold into wet mixture, along with vanilla and nuts. Turn batter into prepared pans. Bake 1 hour, or until tester comes out clean. Yield: 3 loaves.

Pat Chappell, Host
BED & BREAKFAST OF PHILADELPHIA, PENNSYLVANIA

Peach Bread

1/2 cup butter or margarine, softened
1 cup sugar
3 eggs
2¾ cups all-purpose flour
1½ teaspoons baking powder
1 teaspoon salt
1/2 teaspoon baking soda
1½ teaspoons cinnamon
2 cups sliced fresh peaches*
1/2 cup orange juice
1 teaspoon vanilla

Preheat oven to 350°. Grease and flour a 9-inch loaf pan. Cream butter in mixing bowl. Gradually add sugar, combining well. Add eggs, 1 at a time, beating well after each addition. Combine flour, baking powder, salt, soda and cinnamon. Stir into creamed mixture alternately with peaches, beginning and ending with dry mixture. Add orange juice and vanilla, mixing well. Pour batter into prepared pan and bake 1 hour or longer, until done. Yield: 1 loaf.

Barbara Feakes, Host
"TOWNRY FARM"
BERKSHIRE BED & BREAKFAST, MASSACHUSETTS

■ *Easy peach peel: Place whole peach in rapidly boiling water for 15 seconds, then into an ice cold water bath. All the "fuzzies" will disappear faster.

"Pick A Preserve" Bread

1 cup margarine
1½ cups sugar
1 teaspoon vanilla
1/4 teaspoon lemon extract
4 eggs
3 cups all-purpose flour
1 teaspoon salt
1 teaspoon cream of tartar
1/2 teaspoon baking soda
1 cup jam (strawberry, currant, marmalade or personal favorite)
1/2 cup sour cream
1 cup chopped nuts

Preheat oven to 350°. Cream margarine, sugar, vanilla and lemon extract in large mixing bowl until fluffy. Add eggs, one at a time, beating well after each addition. Sift together flour, salt, cream of tartar and soda; set aside. Combine jam, sour cream and nuts; add to creamed mixture alternately with dry ingredients. Pour batter into three greased 5-inch loaf pans. Bake 50 to 55 minutes. Yield: 3 loaves.

Veronica LaRoy, Host
BETSY ROSS BED & BREAKFAST, MICHIGAN

Pioneer Wheat Bread

2 packages active dry yeast
1/3 cup warm water
1 tablespoon cooking oil
1 tablespoon salt
1 tablespoon honey
1 tablespoon molasses
3 cups milk, scalded, cooled
6 cups whole wheat flour (approximately)

Soften yeast in warm water. Add oil, salt, honey, molasses, cooled milk and blend. Add enough flour to make soft dough that leaves sides of pan (may be a little sticky). Turn onto floured surface and knead 5 to 10 minutes. Shape into 2 loaves; place in greased 7-inch loaf pans. Allow to rise not quite double in bulk (1½ to 2 hours) and bake in 375° oven for 45 minutes or until tests done. Yield: 2 loaves.

This is especially easy because it is mixed, kneaded and shaped into loaves all at one time. (Use 1 package yeast at high altitude.) From *Famous Mormon Recipes* by Winnifred Jardine, published by Liddle Enterprises, Inc., Box 8657, Salt Lake City, Utah 84104.

BED 'N' BREAKFAST ASSOCIATION OF UTAH

St. Louis Bran Bread

1 cup bran cereal (nuggets or buds)
1 cup brown sugar, firmly packed
1 cup buttermilk
1 cup all-purpose flour
1 teaspoon baking soda
1/2 cup raisins
1/2 cup chopped nuts

Preheat oven to 325°. Grease two 7-inch loaf pans. Combine cereal, sugar, milk, flour, soda, raisins and nuts, mixing well. Fill each pan with half the batter. Bake 50 minutes to 1 hour. Cool and slice. Yield: 2 loaves.

GATEWAY BED & BREAKFAST, MISSOURI

Tropical Island Fruit Bread

1 papaya or mango, peeled, mashed*
2 eggs
1/4 cup oil
1/2 cup honey
1 teaspoon lemon juice
2 cups whole wheat flour
1 teaspoon baking soda
1/2 teaspoon salt
1 cup chopped nuts
1 cup raisins

Preheat oven to 350°. Grease two 9-inch loaf pans. Place mashed fruit in large mixing bowl. Add eggs, oil, honey and lemon juice, mixing to combine well. Sift together flour, baking soda and salt. Stir into fruit mixture, until well moistened. Turn batter into prepared pans and bake 45 to 55 minutes. Yield: 2 loaves.

*If out of season, 3 to 4 bananas can be substituted for fruit.

Evie Warner
BED & BREAKFAST HAWAII

■ *To judge ripeness of papayas and mangoes, press gently. If they yield to pressure, finger they're ready to slice, peel and seed for Evie's quick and easy bread.

Whole Wheat Herb Bread

2 packages dry yeast
1/4 cup warm water
1/4 cup sugar or honey
1/4 cup butter or margarine
2 teaspoons salt
1 cup milk, scalded
2 eggs
1/4 teaspoon basil
1/4 teaspoon thyme
1/4 teaspoon oregano
1/2 teaspoon nutmeg
3 cups bread flour
2 cups whole wheat flour

Dissolve yeast in warm water. Mix sugar, butter and salt in large bowl. Stir in scalded milk; set aside to cool to lukewarm. Blend in dissolved yeast, eggs, basil, thyme, oregano and nutmeg.

Alternately beat in enough bread and whole wheat flours to make a soft dough. Turn out onto floured board or pastry cloth and knead 10 minutes. Put dough into a buttered bowl, cover and let rise until doubled in bulk, about 1½ to 2 hours.

Punch down dough and divide in half. Form into loaves and place into two greased 9-inch pans. Let rise to edge of pans. Bake in preheated 350° oven 35 to 40 minutes, or until well browned. Yield: 2 loaves.

Pat Wells, Host
BED & BREAKFAST OF PHILADELPHIA, PENNSYLVANIA

Caramel Biscuit Ring-A-Round

1/3 cup brown sugar, firmly packed
3 tablespoons butter or margarine
1 tablespoon water
1/3 cup chopped nuts
1 can (8 ounces) refrigerator biscuits

Combine brown sugar, butter and water in a 1-quart round glass baking dish. Microwave* on medium (5) for 2 to 4 minutes, until butter is melted. Stir in nuts. Separate biscuits. Add biscuits to butter mixture, stirring to coat each piece. Push biscuits and coating to sides of dish and place a glass, open end up, in center.

Microwave† on medium (5), 6 to 8 minutes, rotating dish 1/2 turn after 3 minutes. Remove biscuits from microwave when no longer doughy. Let stand 2 minutes. Twist glass out and invert biscuit ring onto serving plate, allowing dish to stay over top a few minutes to allow all the glaze to drip off. Yield: 6 servings.

Serve warm with forks to pull sections apart into individual servings. Recipe can be frozen and reheated just before serving.

*For conventional oven, place in preheated 400° oven until butter melts.
†For conventional oven, use an oven-proof glass in the center, and then bake 10 to 15 minutes.

Carol Hart
FLORIDA SUNCOAST BED AND BREAKFAST, FLORIDA

MUFFINS

The muffin man, the muffin man, goes the childhood rhyme. In today's B&B business, muffins are a true home-baked specialty. Thrifty hosts serve muffins, fresh and quickly down the tummy; two days old, split, buttered and bubbling from the broiler; stale, finely crumbled, tin-stored for use in pie shells, toppings and breads; or as a last resort, bird food! As you can see, B&B hosts waste not a crumb.

Each of these recipes may be used from sunrise to sunset, transforming a continental repast into a gourmet meal!

Coffee Bran Muffins

■ A great way to use this morning's leftover coffee for tomorrow's tasty muffins.

3/4 cup all-purpose flour
2 teaspoons baking powder
1/2 teaspoon salt
1/2 teaspoon cinnamon
1 cup unprocessed bran
1/2 cup cold, strong coffee
1 tablespoon butter, melted
1/2 cup superfine sugar
1 egg, beaten
1 tablespoon raisins, finely chopped

Preheat oven to 400°. Grease or line 8 muffin cups. In medium-size mixing bowl, sift together flour, baking powder, salt and cinnamon. Stir in bran. Combine coffee, butter, sugar and egg, stirring to blend well.

Gradually pour liquid mixture into dry ingredients, stirring constantly, but being careful not to over-beat. Fold in raisins. Spoon batter evenly into prepared muffin cups. Bake 15 minutes. Yield: 8 muffins.*

*Recipe doubles well.

Betty Cordellos
NASHVILLE BED & BREAKFAST, TENNESSEE

Comfort Crescents

1 cup cold margarine, or 1/2 cup margarine and 1/2 cup butter
2 cups all-purpose flour
1 egg yolk
3/4 cup sour cream
3/4 cup sugar
1 tablespoon cinnamon
1 cup finely chopped walnuts

Cut margarine into flour until consistency of coarse meal. Blend in egg and sour cream. Shape dough into a ball, roll in wax paper and refrigerate 4 hours.

When ready to use, cut dough into quarters. Roll each quarter into a 12-inch circle. Combine sugar, cinnamon and walnuts, sprinkling each circle with 1/4 the mixture, to within 1/2 inch of edges. Cut each circle into 8 pie-shaped wedges (should be about 4 inches at larger end).

Starting at wider edge, carefully roll up, jelly-roll style, turning ends toward each other to form crescent. Place crescents on ungreased cookie sheets, with point of horns on the bottom. Bake in preheated 375° oven, 25 minutes. Remove to rack to cool.* Yield: 32 crescents.

*Sprinkle with additional cinnamon sugar while warm, if desired. Keeps well in a covered tin.

Ann Mahoney, Host
SOUTHERN COMFORT BED &
BREAKFAST RESERVATION SERVICE, LOUISIANA

Popovers With Cheese

2 eggs
1 cup milk
1 cup all-purpose flour
1/2 teaspoon salt
Grated Parmesan cheese

Grease a 12-cup muffin tin. Place in refrigerator to chill. Break eggs into medium-size bowl. Add milk, flour and salt, mixing well. Batter will be lumpy.

Fill muffin cups 3/4 full. Sprinkle top of batter with cheese. Put in COLD oven, turn oven to 450° and bake for 20 to 30 minutes. DO NOT open oven door for 20 minutes. Yield: 12 popovers.

Daryl Mooney
"CHENEY HOUSE," NEW HAMPSHIRE

Iron Skillet Biscuits

"We are pleased to share the favorite breakfast item of the 'Flint Street Inn.' We serve a full Southern-style breakfast and have to include a basket of hot, homemade biscuits. I use my grandmother's iron skillet for baking. I would like to think that it is responsible for the biscuits turning out every time, but I know it's just that I enjoy the pleasure of using it.

"Since mornings are so busy, I must have a recipe that is simple and good. The solution—drop biscuits, which we call Iron Skillet Biscuits."

    2 cups self-rising flour
    3/4 cup milk, buttermilk or water
    3 tablespoons shortening
    1/2 cup butter, melted

Preheat oven to 475°. Place flour in large mixing bowl and cut in shortening until crumb stage. Gradually add milk and stir until flour is moistened. (If using buttermilk, add 3/4 teaspoon baking soda to milk before adding to mixture.) Generously grease a 10-inch skillet.

Using a large tablespoon* as a measure, scoop out a heaping amount of dough. Using another spoon, push dough off into skillet. Place skillet in oven. Remove skillet from oven within 5 minutes and brush biscuits with melted butter. Return to oven and continue baking until they are golden brown, 10 to 15 minutes. Yield: 8 to 12 biscuits.

"This recipe never fails, and is guaranteed to please."

Rick and Lynne Vogel
"Flint Street Inn," North Carolina

■ *A good time to use your ice cream scoop!

Maine Blueberry Muffins

1/4 cup butter
1/2 cup sugar
1 large egg
1 teaspoon grated lemon rind
2 cups all-purpose flour
4 teaspoons baking powder
1/2 teaspoon salt
1/4 teaspoon nutmeg
1 cup milk
1 cup blueberries
Cinnamon sugar (optional)

Cream butter and sugar, beat in egg and lemon rind. Sift together flour, baking powder, salt and nutmeg; add to creamed mixture, alternately with milk. Gently fold in berries. Bake in greased muffin tins at 375° for about 20 minutes. Yield: 1 dozen lovely, "cakey" muffins.

Sally B. Godfrey
BED & BREAKFAST DOWN EAST, LTD., MAINE

■ For browner tops, sprinkle with cinnamon sugar before baking.

Maple Applesauce Muffins

2 cups all-purpose flour
1 tablespoon baking powder
1 teaspoon salt
1/2 teaspoon cinnamon
1/2 cup butter or margarine
1/4 cup sugar
3/4 cup maple syrup
2 eggs, lightly beaten
3/4 cup applesauce

Preheat oven to 375°. Grease a 12-cup muffin tin. Sift together flour, baking powder, salt and cinnamon; set aside. In large bowl, cream shortening and sugar, until fluffy. Add maple syrup. Stir in eggs and applesauce. Combine with flour mixture and stir well. Fill prepared muffin tins 2/3 full and bake for 20 minutes. Yield: 1 dozen.

Terri Pierce, Host
AMERICAN BED & BREAKFAST, VERMONT

California Orange Muffins

1 large orange
2¼ cups all-purpose flour
1/2 cup sugar
1/4 teaspoon salt
2½ teaspoons baking powder
1/2 teaspoon baking soda
1 egg
1/2 cup milk
1/4 cup butter, melted
1/4 cup confectioners' sugar

Preheat oven to 425°. Finely grate zest (rind) of orange. Cut orange in half, squeeze juice and reserve. Sift flour, sugar, salt, baking powder and soda together into large bowl. Stir in zest. Beat orange juice, egg, milk and butter together. Mix lightly into dry ingredients. Generously grease a 12-cup muffin tin. Fill each cup 3/4 full. Sprinkle batter with confectioners' sugar. Bake approximately 20 minutes, or until lightly browned. Yield: 1 dozen.

Bob Williams, Chef
GRAMMA'S BED & BREAKFAST, CALIFORNIA

Peanut Butter Surprise Muffins

■ Children love these. Use your leftover jams and jellies of different flavors, letting guests choose their own peanut butter and jelly combo.

1 egg, lightly beaten
1 cup milk
1/2 cup crunchy peanut butter
3 tablespoons vegetable oil
1½ cups waffle-type cereal (rice, corn or wheat)
1 cup all-purpose flour
1/3 cup sugar
2 teaspoons baking powder
1/4 teaspoon salt
1/3 cup jam or preserves

Preheat oven to 400°. Grease or line a 12-cup muffin tin. Combine egg, milk, peanut butter and oil in medium-size bowl. Stir in cereal and let stand 5 minutes. In large bowl, sift together flour, sugar, baking powder and salt.

Stir in cereal mixture, until thoroughly moistened. Fill muffin cups 1/3 full. Drop 1 teaspoon of jam on each, carefully, not touching sides of pan or liner. Cover with batter to 3/4 full. Bake 20 to 25 minutes, until golden brown. Yield: 1 dozen.

Barbara Fredholm
MID-MISSOURI BED AND BREAKFAST, MISSOURI

Poppy Seed Muffins

3/4 cup sugar
1/4 cup butter or margarine, softened
1/2 teaspoon grated orange peel
2 eggs
2 cups all-purpose flour
2½ teaspoons baking powder
1/2 teaspoon salt
1/4 teaspoon nutmeg
1 cup milk
1/2 cup golden raisins
1/2 cup chopped pecans
1 can (1⅝ ounces) poppy seeds

Preheat oven to 400°. In mixing bowl, cream together sugar, butter and orange peel. Add eggs, one at a time, beating well after each addition. Sift together flour, baking powder, salt and nutmeg. Add flour to creamed mixture, alternately with milk, beating well after each addition. Fold in raisins, nuts and poppy seeds. Fill lined muffin pans 3/4 full. Bake about 20 minutes. Yield: 16 muffins.

Marlene Van Lent
BED & BREAKFAST OF NEBRASKA

Rhubarb-Strawberry Muffins

1¾ cups flour
1/2 cup sugar
2½ teaspoons baking powder
Dash of salt
1 egg, lightly beaten
3/4 cup milk
1/3 cup vegetable oil
1 teaspoon vanilla
1 teaspoon grated orange peel
3/4 cup diced rhubarb*
1/2 cup sliced strawberries

2 tablespoons brown sugar
1/4 teaspoon cinnamon

Preheat oven to 400°. Grease two 12-cup muffin tins. Sift flour, sugar, baking powder and salt into large bowl. Combine egg, milk, oil, vanilla and orange peel in small bowl. Pour egg mixture into dry ingredients and stir with fork until moistened. Fold in rhubarb and sliced strawberries. Fill muffin cups 2/3 full.

For topping, combine brown sugar and cinnamon. Sprinkle evenly over batter. Bake for 20 to 25 minutes. Yield: 2 dozen.

Daryl Mooney
"CHENEY HOUSE," NEW HAMPSHIRE

■ *Stewed or diced frozen rhubarb works well, when fresh rhubarb is unavailable. Enhance flavor by adding 1 teaspoon strawberry essence to batter.

"We fondly refer to the host who serves fresh fruit and homemade raisin bran muffins as 'Ms. Regularity.' It is her philosophy that travelers often get 'bogged down,' and it's her attempt to improve the health, as well as the mood, of her guests."

Kate Peterson
BED & BREAKFAST ROCKY MOUNTAINS, COLORADO

Six Weeks Bran Muffins

5 cups all-purpose flour
5 teaspoons baking soda
2 teaspoons salt
6 cups bran cereal nuggets
2 cups boiling water
1 cup vegetable oil
3 cups sugar
4 eggs, beaten
1 quart buttermilk
2 cups raisins

Sift flour, baking soda and salt together; set aside. Place 2 cups bran cereal into bowl, cover with boiling water and set aside. In your largest mixing bowl, combine remaining bran cereal, oil, sugar, eggs and buttermilk. Add flour mixture and stir well. Add soaked bran and mix until well combined. Fold in raisins. Cover and store* in refrigerator up to 6 weeks. Yield: 12 cups batter.

To bake, preheat oven to 400°. Grease desired number of muffin cups and fill each 2/3 full. Bake 20 minutes.

Pecans, with the raisins, are good, too.

John Collins, Host
BED & BREAKFAST BIRMINGHAM, INC., ALABAMA

■ *Store batter in a covered pitcher for ready-to-pour convenience. Date your container so you know when you made this batter and when you must finish using it. For the other five weeks, let your morning mood determine which fruits and nuts you want to add to your batter.

Grandma Tintera's Siska

Try these Czechoslovakian doughnuts for a special breakfast treat. "One day of baking makes many days of good eating with these Czechoslovakian doughnuts. I press my thumb through the center of each siska before frying, to make an indentation for the filling. These doughnuts freeze well, and can be taken out of the freezer two hours before needed, warmed in a toaster oven, then topped with your favorite jams or Prune Butter." (See this chapter, *Spreads* page 70.)

    1 package dry yeast
    1/2 cup water
    1 tablespoon sugar
    1/4 cup margarine
    1/3 cup sugar
    1 teaspoon salt
    1 egg
    2 tablespoons grated lemon peel
    4 cups all-purpose flour
    1 cup milk
    Vegetable oil

Dissolve yeast in water with 1 tablespoon sugar. Cream margarine, 1/3 cup sugar and the salt together in large mixing bowl. Add egg and lemon peel. Stir in flour, a little at a time, alternating with milk and yeast mixture, and mixing well after each addition. Shape dough into a large ball, place in lightly greased bowl, turn once to grease, and set aside to rise for 2½ hours.

Roll out dough to 1/2 inch thick. Cut with biscuit cutter. Fry in 3 inches of oil at 375° until golden to dark brown. Remove from oil and place on cooling rack. Yield: About 3 dozen.

Pam Edson, Host
BETSY ROSS BED & BREAKFAST, MISSOURI

COFFEE CAKES

Breakfast tea cakes are as traditional as the B&B concept. Served as a daily morning delicacy, for Sunday pastoral visits, or afternoon teatime, the offering of coffee cakes remains the same: A sweet morsel to dunk and have conversation over!

Warmed coffee cakes, buns and special toasts make breakfast, brunch, or coffee-klatching an occasion.

The following recipes contain a selection for everyone. Some are fancy enough for holidays; others require patience, time and gentleness; some are mixed in minutes from packaged goods. The making and tasting choices are yours!

Cinnamon Milk Sticks

■ Quick and easy for a last-minute breakfast treat. And children love these for a snack any time!

> 1 loaf (1 pound) unsliced bread
> 1/2 cup sugar
> 1 teaspoon cinnamon
> 1 cup evaporated milk
> 4 tablespoons butter, melted

Cut six 1-inch slices from loaf. Remove crusts, and cut each piece into 3 strips. Combine sugar and cinnamon; place on wax paper. Dip each strip into milk, brush with butter and roll in sugar and cinnamon. Lay strips in shallow oven-proof pan. Bake at 400° about 20 minutes. Remove from oven when browned to your liking. Yield: 18.

Peg Marshall
BED AND BREAKFAST OF LOS ANGELES, CALIFORNIA

Flaky Prune Turnovers

1 package pie crust mix
1/2 cup sour cream
1 cup finely chopped prunes
1/4 cup sugar*
1/2 cup water
1/4 cup finely chopped walnuts
1 teaspoon lemon juice
2 tablespoons sugar*
1/4 teaspoon cinnamon
1/4 teaspoon nutmeg

With a fork, stir pie crust mix and sour cream together until well blended. Form into ball, cover and refrigerate.

Combine prunes, 1/4 cup sugar and water in saucepan. Bring to a boil and cook 15 minutes. Stir in walnuts and lemon juice. Remove from heat and set aside to cool. Divide dough into 8 portions. Roll out each portion into a 6-inch circle on a floured board. Place 2 tablespoons prune mixture on 1/2 of each circle. Fold pastry over and seal. Vent tops of pastry and place on ungreased cookie sheets. Combine 2 tablespoons of sugar, cinnamon and nutmeg; gently sprinkle over pastry tops. Bake in 400° preheated oven, approximately 15 minutes, or until lightly brown. Yield: 8.

* Omit sugar for diabetic recipe.

GATEWAY BED & BREAKFAST, MISSOURI

■ For well-stuffed turnovers, double filling mixture!

Glazed Prune Cake

"I make this without the glaze to serve as a coffee cake, but it also makes a delicious dessert with the glaze."

Batter:
2 cups sugar
1 cup oil
3 eggs
1 cup dried prunes, cooked
2 cups all-purpose flour
1 teaspoon cinnamon
1 teaspoon nutmeg
1 teaspooon ground cloves
1/2 teaspoon salt
1 cup buttermilk
1 teaspoon baking soda
1/2 teaspoon almond extract
1/2 teaspoon vanilla
1/2 cup chopped nuts

Glaze (Optional):
1/2 cup buttermilk
1/2 teaspoon soda
1/2 teaspoon vanilla
1 cup sugar
1½ cups butter

Preheat oven to 350°. Oil a 10-inch tube pan. In a large bowl, mix together sugar, oil, eggs and prunes. Sift flour with spices into another bowl. Dissolve soda in buttermilk. Add dry ingredients to egg mixture alternately with buttermilk. Beat well. Add almond and vanilla extracts and stir in nuts. Pour into prepared tube pan and bake for 1 hour. Yield: 8 to 10 servings.

To prepare glaze, simmer all ingredients in a small saucepan for 10 minutes. Pour over cake while cake is still hot. Cool and remove from pan.

Sue Carroll
THE MAINSTAY, NEW JERSEY

Iowa Honey Buns

3¼ cups all-purpose flour
1 package dry yeast
1 cup milk
1/4 cup honey
1/4 cup shortening
1 teaspoon salt
1 egg

Honey Butter:
1/2 cup butter
1/3 cup honey
1 teaspoon cinnamon

Topping:
1/2 cup honey
1/3 cup brown sugar
3 tablespoons butter
1 cup chopped pecans

Mix 1¾ cups flour with yeast in a large bowl. In a saucepan, heat milk with 1/4 cup honey, the shortening and salt, until lukewarm (115 to 120°). Add warm liquids to flour mixture. Beat in egg and remaining flour. Shape dough into a ball and place in a greased bowl. Cover and let rise until double in bulk (approximately 1½ hours).

Meanwhile, prepare honey butter by beating butter, honey and cinnamon together until well mixed. Set aside.

Prepare topping shortly before dough will be ready. Combine honey, brown sugar and butter in saucepan. Heat and stir until butter and sugar are melted.

When dough has doubled, divide in half. Roll each half into a 12- by 8-inch rectangle. Spread each rectangle with half the honey butter. Starting at wide end, roll up each rectangle jelly-roll fashion. Cut each into twelve 1-inch slices.

Divide topping between two greased 8-inch square pans. Sprinkle with pecans. Place slices, cut side down, into pans. Let rise until double. Bake in preheated 375° oven, 25 to 30 minutes. Cool in pans for 5 minutes. Then place wax paper under cooling rack and invert rolls onto rack. Remove pans. Yield: 2 dozen.

Janet Ryan
BED & BREAKFAST in IOWA, LTD.

Kansas City Coffee Cake

2 packages yeast
1/4 cup warm water
2¼ cups all-purpose flour
2 tablespoons sugar
1 teaspoon salt
1/2 cup butter
1 egg
1/4 cup evaporated milk
1/4 cup raisins
1/4 cup butter, softened
1/2 cup brown sugar
1 teaspoon cinnamon

Glaze:
1½ tablespoons butter
3/4 cup confectioners' sugar
1/2 teaspoon vanilla
1/2 to 1 tablespoon evaporated milk

Soften yeast in warm water; set aside. Sift together flour, sugar and salt. Cut in butter. Add yeast, egg, evaporated milk; mix well. Stir in raisins. Chill at least 3 hours.

Divide dough in half. On floured surface roll out into rectangles. Spread with butter, brown sugar and cinnamon. Roll up jelly-roll style. Shape into crescents. Divide into 6 pieces, but don't cut all the way through. Let rise 45 minutes to 1 hour. Bake at 350° for 13 to 15 minutes.

Mix glaze ingredients and spread over cakes. Yield: 2 cakes (12 slices).

Dale and Diane Kuhn
KANSAS CITY BED & BREAKFAST, KANSAS

No-Salt Coffee Cake

■ B&B hosts try to cater to the eating habits and special dietary needs of their guests. For hosts and guests looking for a salt-free, delicious breakfast sweet, this easy "do-in-minutes" coffee cake is for you.

2 cups all-purpose flour
1½ cups sugar
3/4 cup butter or margarine
2 eggs
3/4 cup milk or orange juice
2 teaspoons baking powder
Cinnamon
Butter

Preheat oven to 400°. Grease two 8-inch round cake pans. In a large bowl, mix flour, sugar and butter by hand. Reserve 3/4 cup of mixture for crumb topping. To remainder of batter, add eggs, milk and baking powder, mixing thoroughly.

Divide batter into pans and top with reserved crumb mixture. Sprinkle with cinnamon and dot with butter. Bake 15 minutes. Yield: 8 to 12 servings.

Ann Magagna
BED AND BREAKFAST OF THE
POCONOS-NORTHEAST, PENNSYLVANIA

Old-Fashioned Scones

2 cups all-purpose flour
3 teaspoons baking powder
4 tablespoons sugar
1/2 teaspoon salt
4 tablespoons butter or margarine
2 eggs
1/2 cup heavy whipping cream
1/2 cup raisins (optional)

Sift together flour, baking powder, 2 tablespoons sugar and salt in large bowl. Cut in butter to consistency of course meal. Form a well in center of mixture.

Separate one egg, reserving the white. Beat yolk and remaining whole egg together, blending in cream. Fold in raisins if desired. Pour cream mixture into well; stir with a fork until dough pulls away from sides of bowl. Preheat oven to 400°.

Turn dough onto a floured surface; knead about 10 times. Divide dough in half. Roll each section into a 6-inch circle, each about 1 inch thick. Cut circles into 4 wedges.* Place about 1 inch apart on ungreased cookie sheets. Brush tops with reserved egg white; sprinkle with remaining sugar. Bake 15 minutes. Yield: 8 servings.

Patrick and Jill O'Neill, Hosts
"CALIFORNIA ADVENTURE B&B"
HOME SUITE HOMES, CALIFORNIA

■ *Or use traditional cutting method, crimping edges with pie crimper. Other designs can be made by using antique cookie cutters. Then sprinkle scones with colored sugar.

Pennsylvania Dutch Crumb Cake

6 cups all-purpose flour
2 cups brown sugar
2 cups sugar
2 teaspoons salt
2 teaspoons baking powder
1 cup margarine
4 eggs
2 cups buttermilk
2 teaspoons baking soda

Preheat oven to 375°. Grease and lightly flour four 8-inch round cake pans. Combine flour, sugars, salt and baking powder in large mixing bowl. Cut in margarine, and rub ingredients together until they resemble fine crumbs. Set aside 2 cups crumbs for topping.

Add eggs, buttermilk and baking soda to remaining crumb mixture; mix well with rotary beater. Spread batter in prepared pans. Sprinkle with reserved crumb topping. Bake 25 to 30 minutes, or until toothpick inserted in center comes out clean. Yield: 32 servings.

Marigrace Komarnicki, Host
BED & BREAKFAST OF PHILADELPHIA, PENNSYLVANIA

Sister's Coffee Cake

3 cups all-purpose flour
2 cups sugar
1 teaspoon baking powder
1 teaspoon nutmeg
1 teaspoon cloves
1 teaspoon cinnamon
1 teaspoon salt
1 cup shortening
1 teaspoon baking soda
2 cups buttermilk or sour milk

Preheat oven to 350°. Sift flour, sugar, baking powder, nutmeg, cloves, cinnamon and salt together into medium bowl. Cut in shortening. Reserve 1 cup of mixture for topping.* Add baking soda and buttermilk to remaining mixture. Pour batter into a greased 9- by 13- by 2-inch oven-proof pan, or two 8-inch square pans. Bake 45 to 60 minutes. Yield: 8 to 12 servings.

*I often do this much the night before, if I plan to serve it for breakfast.

Pat Reese, Host
BED & BREAKFAST INTERNATIONAL, CALIFORNIA

Creamy Olive Spread

6 ounces cream cheese, softened
1/2 cup mayonnaise
1 cup chopped salad olives (reserve liquid)
1/2 cup chopped pecans
2 tablespoons reserved olive liquid
Dash pepper*

Blend cheese, mayonnaise, olives, nuts, liquid and pepper together. Cover and chill for 24 hours before using. Yield: 2½ cups.

"Spread on party rye slices."

Norma Buzan
BETSY ROSS BED & BREAKFAST, MISSOURI

■ *For added spice try using cayenne pepper, a dash of Tabasco and 2 drops of Worcestershire sauce.

Grape Jelly (Muscadine)

"Around here, in the Ozark areas, we *love* Muscadine (pronounced musk-ah-dine) grape jelly. You hafta fight chiggers, ticks, snakes and *heat* to pick 'em, 'cause they're better grown in the forest, than cultivated. Consequently, the people brave enough to pick these little jewels charge an arm and a leg for them, but rightly so. It's best to have these slightly ahead of full ripeness—they're not so squashy.

"Wash your grapes well, after stemming. Put in a kettle with a little bit of water (about 5 parts grapes to 1 part water) and, Granny says, add a cut-up apple—saves them from getting too sugary. Boil gently 'til they are soft. Strain through jelly bag, or line a sieve or colander with clean tea towel, and let drip long enough to leave just skins and pulp in bag (sometimes this is overnight). Then follow any recipe on a pectin package. Use the leftover pulp to make Grape Conserve (follow any pectin recipe for fruit butter)."

B. C. Jett
OZARK B&B, ARKANSAS

Green Pepper Jelly

2 cups ground green peppers (about 6 large)
6½ cups sugar
1½ cups white vinegar
1 bottle (6 ounces) fruit pectin
1½ teaspoons crushed red pepper or Tabasco sauce
3 drops green food coloring (optional)

Sterilize four 8-ounce jelly glasses. Keep in hot water until ready to use.

Combine peppers, sugar and vinegar in a 3-quart saucepan, and boil for 3 minutes. Remove from heat. Let stand for 5 minutes, then strain, if desired. Add food coloring. Ladle into jelly glasses, leaving 1/2 inch clearing at top. Cool and cover with aluminum foil and lids, or use liquid paraffin. Yield: 4 cups.

"Delicious canapes when crackers are spread with cream cheese and topped with this jelly."

Vanza Lazet, Host
BED & BREAKFAST OF PHILADELPHIA, PENNSYLVANIA

Highbush Cranberry Jelly

"The highbush cranberry is actually not a member of the cranberry family, but it has a similar tart flavor; the berries hang in clusters from shrubs that are generally 5 to 10 feet in height. The bright red berries are best picked after a few mellowing frosts, but before the first hard freeze."

>   2 cups washed berries
>   3 cups water
>   1 or more packages Sure-Jell
>   4 cups sugar

Place the berries in water and bring to a boil, mashing them as they cook. Simmer for 5 minutes, then strain. Add 1 package of Sure-Jell to each 6 cups of juice and bring to a full boil. Add sugar and bring to a full rolling boil. Boil hard for 1 minute. Ladle into sterilized containers. Yield: 6 cups.

>   "The jelly has a lovely color and an equally attractive, unique flavor."
>   Tom and Julie Davis, Hosts
>   BED & BREAKFAST GUEST-HOMES, WISCONSIN

Prune Butter

"This is the great butter that we serve with Grandma Tintera's Siska. (See this chapter, *Muffins*, page 60.)

>   1 pound pitted prunes
>   1 cup water
>   1 teaspoon lemon juice

Cook prunes in small saucepan with water, until very soft. With spoon stir lemon juice into prunes until well blended.* Set aside to cool before covering. Yield: 1½ cups.

>   Pam Edson, Host
>   BETSY ROSS BED & BREAKFAST, MICHIGAN

■ *You can also stir in 1/4 cup butter and 1/2 teaspoon cinnamon.

Spring Butter

3/4 cup butter, room temperature
2 tablespoons minced parsley
1 tablespoon snipped chives
1 tablespoon lemon juice, room temperature
Salt and pepper to taste

In a small bowl, cream together all ingredients. Cover and allow to stand at room temperature at least 1 hour before using on wheat breads, etc. Keeps well in refrigerator for 1 to 2 weeks. Yield: About 3/4 cup.

Gloria Lyon, Host
"AMERICAN FAMILY INN"
BED & BREAKFAST SAN FRANCISCO, CALIFORNIA

Tomato Marmalade

About 8 pounds firm, ripe tomatoes
4 oranges, sliced, seeded and cut up
4 lemons, sliced, seeded and cut up
2 teaspoons, cinnamon
1 tablespoon whole cloves
*Sugar

Put each whole tomato on fork, dip into boiling, then chilled water; remove skin, chop roughly and measure into quart container. Measure 4 quarts of tomatoes and let stand. Place cut up oranges and lemons in large kettle with cinnamon and cloves. Pour off most of the tomato liquid and discard (or use in soups). Add tomatoes to orange and lemon mixture in kettle.

*Add 1 cup of sugar for each cup of tomatoes. Bring to a boil, stir to dissolve sugar. Boil, stirring to prevent burning, until marmalade "sheets" off spoon, or registers 220° on a candy thermometer. Ladle into hot sterile jars and seal. Yield: about eighteen 6-ounce jars.

Sally B. Godfrey
BED & BREAKFAST DOWN EAST, LTD., MAINE

Breakfast and Brunch

III

Breakfast and Brunch (Entrees)

LIKE the cable on a sailing ship, which runs from the mainmast to support it, the following recipes are the "stabilizing influence" of the meal, whether it be breakfast, brunch or dinner. They include such staples as eggs, fish, poultry and meats. B&B hosts have carefully honed these recipes from their favorites. Some can be made in advance; all can be increased or decreased easily as you need. Cooked via slowpot, oven or stove top, these recipes fit any occasion or any taste, to portray the variety and great tradition of regional entrees.

EGGS AND CHEESE DISHES

FIRST, last and always, eggs and cheese play a part in the cast of traditional foods and occasions. With 12-hour prior preparation for many of these recipes, their convenience and ease are a welcome aid to any busy host.

Strata and quiche provide hearty breakfast dishes to greet the punctual guest, yet keep well to await the late arrival. The herbs and spices lend an enticing aroma. Also, these dishes advance to the supper or dinner table with little ado.

Some of the following recipes from neighboring countries exemplify the delectable tastes that appeal to the educated palate. Rely on these dishes often as they contribute their share to the excitement and ambience of after-theatre dinner parties, holiday to-do's, patio impromptus, picnics and family get-togethers!

Asparagus Supreme Omelet

"1983 Asparagus Festival winner. . . We love this recipe and often leave out the meat and add alfalfa sprouts and tomatoes."

    3 tablespoons butter, melted
    1/4 cup chopped green pepper
    1 tablespoon diced onion
    1/4 cup cooked asparagus, cut into small pieces
    2 slices bacon, fried, drained and crumbled
    1 smoked link sausage, fried and sliced
    3 slices processed cheese
    1 tablespoon butter
    3 eggs
    2 tablespoons water
    Salt and pepper to taste
    Asparagus spears, cooked (optional)
    Parsley (optional)

Prepare filling by combining 3 tablespoons butter, green pepper, onion, asparagus, bacon and sausage in a small bowl. Set cheese aside.

Heat 1 tablespoon butter in 10-inch skillet or omelet pan. Beat together eggs, water, salt and pepper. Pour into pan, tilting to spread liquid. Cook gently and sprinkle the filling mixture across the center, edge to edge. Top with cheese slices. Flip one side of the egg mixture over the center, then flip the other side over. Decorate with asparagus spears and parsley, if desired. Yield: 2 servings.

Pam Edson, Host
Betsy Ross B&B, Michigan

Barbara's Blue Cheese Quiche

1 9-inch frozen pie shell
4 ounces blue cheese, crumbled
1½ cups low-fat cottage cheese
1/4 cup butter, softened
1/2 teaspoon salt
4 eggs, well beaten
Dash cayenne pepper
1/4 cup chopped onion, firmly packed
Chopped chives

Preheat oven to 400°. Prick pie shell and bake for 12 to 15 minutes, until golden. Remove pie shell and reduce oven heat to 350°.

Cream together cheeses and butter. Mix in salt, eggs, cayenne and onion. Pour into prepared pie shell. Sprinkle with chives. Bake at 350° for 40 to 45 minutes or until custard is thick. Yield: 4 to 6 servings.

Barbara Hershey
STODDARD COOPER INN, GEORGIA

Barry Goldwater's Arizona Quiche

"Barry Goldwater loves his native state, and Arizona is equally proud of him. When he was a boy he would sit on that enormous hill on which his home is located, and plan to have 'his home' there someday. He runs his own B&B, because of frequent personal guests. As a pilot, he also runs his own CB station from 'his mountain,' and anyone in need can use it to get a message around the world. Barry's quiche, accompanied by Bishop's Loaf [see page 38] and fresh fruit is ready for a dawn breakfast or late brunch in my home."

1 9-inch pie shell, partially baked
1½ cups grated Jack cheese
1 cup grated mild Cheddar cheese
1 can (4 ounces) diced green chilies
1 cup half-and-half
3 eggs, slightly beaten
1/2 teaspoon cumin

Preheat oven to 450°. Bake pie shell for five minutes. Reduce heat to 325°. In small mixing bowl, combine Jack cheese with 1/2 cup Cheddar cheese and spread over pie shell. Sprinkle chilies over cheese. Combine half-and-half, eggs, salt and cumin; pour carefully into pie shell. Top with remaining Cheddar cheese. Bake for 40 to 50 minutes. Yield: 6 servings.

"I gently shake my quiches to test for doneness."

Bessie Lipinski
BED AND BREAKFAST IN ARIZONA

Breakfast Burritos

1 small onion, chopped
3 tablespoons butter
2 tablespoons chopped pimiento
1 can (16 ounces) corn*, drained
1/4 cup green chilies, chopped
2 tablespoons, minced parsley
8 eggs
Salt and pepper to taste
1/2 teaspoon crushed oregano
1 tablespoon butter or margarine
1½ cups grated Jack or Cheddar cheese

4 flour tortillas
Sour cream
Green chili salsa

Saute onion in 3 tablespoons butter until transparent. Add pimiento, corn, chilies and parsley; stir until heated. Beat together eggs, salt, pepper and oregano. Add egg mixture and 1 tablespoon butter to vegetable mixture. Scramble until softly set. Sprinkle with cheese. Set aside and keep warm.

Wrap tortillas in foil and heat in oven or in top of double boiler over medium heat. Remove tortillas and fill with egg mixture. Top each with sour cream and salsa. Yield: 4 servings.

*Substitute 2 cups sauteed, chopped vegetables. Yellow squash, zucchini or carrots work well.

Sally and Dan Campbell
LA CASITA, NEW MEXICO

Cheese Scrambles In Sausage Ring

"We raise our own beef, pigs and poultry; thus our breakfast and brunch menus contain lots of fresh eggs and farm meats. We select foods that are easy to prepare, filling and appealing to both adults and children."

12 eggs
1½ cups milk
1½ cups crushed saltines
1/2 cup chopped onion
1 teaspoon sage (optional)
2 pounds bulk sausage
3 tablespoons butter
3 tablespoons flour
Salt and pepper to taste
1 cup grated Swiss or sharp Cheddar cheese or 1 cup cottage cheese
Green pepper rings
Parsley sprigs
Cherry tomatoes

Preheat oven to 350°. Beat together 2 eggs and 1/2 cup milk. Stir in crackers, onion, sage and sausage. Mix well. To shape mixture, press into a greased 6½-cup ring mold. Unmold into a roasting pan and bake for 50 minutes, draining grease as needed.*

While ring bakes, melt butter in large skillet. Add flour, salt, pepper and remaining 1 cup milk. Cook, stirring for 2 minutes, until bubbly. In large bowl beat remaining 10 eggs with cheese and add to skillet. Scramble until firm, but moist.

Transfer cooked sausage ring to serving platter and spoon scramble eggs into center of ring. Garnish with green pepper rings, parsley sprigs and cherry tomatoes. Yield: 6 generous servings.

Bert and Freya Phillips, Hosts
"GENERAL POTTERS FARM"
REST & REPAST, PENNSYLVANIA

■ *Sausage ring may be baked one day ahead and reheated prior to serving. For large groups fill ring with half Cheese Scrambles and half Clammed Eggs (see next page).

Clammed Eggs

4 eggs
1 tablespoon milk
Salt and pepper to taste
1 can (6½ ounces) clams, whole or chopped, drained
1/2 cup grated Swiss cheese
1 tablespoon butter
2 tablespoons chopped parsley or tarragon

Beat together eggs, milk, salt and pepper. Stir in clams and cheese. Melt butter in a 10-inch skillet. Add egg mixture. Scramble to desired consistency. Sprinkle with herbs. Yield: 2 servings.

Alex Laputz, Host
HOMESTAY B&B, CALIFORNIA

"Simmered sweet onions combined with scrambled eggs, surrounding a mound of sauteed chicken livers on a large platter, is always a hit with my guests. They also enjoy my combination of sauteed onions and sliced mushrooms added to scrambles. . ."

Ruth Sharf, Host
BED & BREAKFAST OF PHILADELPHIA, PENNSYLVANIA

Continental Cheese Bake

1 tablespoon butter
1 cup sliced onion
8 hard-cooked eggs, sliced
2 cups shredded Swiss cheese
1 can (10¾ ounces) cream of mushroom soup
3/4 cup milk
1 teaspoon prepared mustard
1/2 teaspoon seasoned salt
1/4 teaspoon dillweed
1/4 teaspoon pepper
6 slices rye bread, cut into triangles

Preheat oven to 350°. Melt butter in skillet over medium heat. Add onions and cook until tender. Spread onions in an 11½- by 7½-inch baking dish. Top with egg slices; sprinkle with cheese.

Beat together soup, milk, mustard, salt, dill and pepper with a rotary beater, and pour over cheese and eggs. Overlap bread triangles on top of casserole.

Bake for 30 to 35 minutes or until heated through. Place under broiler (5 inches from heat) for 1 minute to toast bread. Yield: 8 servings.

Margaret Breuhan, Host
BETSY ROSS B&B, MICHIGAN

Cottaged Omelet in a Pan

4 eggs, lightly beaten
1 cup low-fat cottage cheese
1 tablespoon chopped chives
Salt and pepper to taste
1 tablespoon sweet butter

Combine eggs, cottage cheese, chives, salt and pepper in a medium size bowl. Melt butter in a fold-over omelet pan.* Divide egg mixture and pour evenly into both sides of pan. Cook until partially set. Close pan and continue cooking for 3 minutes. Flip pan gently and cook approximately 2 more minutes to desired firmness. Yield: 3 generous servings.

Paul Bernard, Host
"AMERICAN FAMILY INN,"
BED AND BREAKFAST SAN FRANCISCO, CALIFORNIA

■ *Flavor is just the same when prepared in a 10-inch skillet. When using a skillet, cover at beginning of cooking time to set top, or finish under broiler.

Egg and Bacon Pie

"This dish was a favorite on an English picnic when I was growing up."

Pastry for 2-crust pie
6 strips bacon, cooked, drained and crumbled
1/2 cup sliced mushrooms
4 large eggs
5 tablespoons milk
1 teaspoon crushed thyme
1 teaspoon minced parsley
Salt and pepper to taste
1 egg white, beaten

Preheat oven to 400°. Line an 8-inch pie plate with half of the pastry. Sprinkle bacon evenly over the pastry and top with mushrooms. Whisk eggs together; stir in milk, thyme and parsley. Add salt and pepper to taste. Pour mixture over bacon and mushrooms.

Dampen edges of pie crust with water and cover with the remaining pastry to form top crust. Pierce the top crust with a fork. Brush crust with beaten egg white. Bake for 10 minutes. Reduce heat to 350° and bake an additional 30 minutes. Yield: 6 servings.

Muriel Collins, Host
BED & BREAKFAST OF PHILADELPHIA, PENNSYLVANIA

Eggs Mornay

2 tablespoons butter
2 tablespoons flour
Dash of Tabasco or Worcestershire sauce
1 teaspoon prepared mustard
2 cups milk
1/3 cup grated Cheddar cheese
6 eggs
Paprika
English muffins

Melt butter in saucepan. Blend in flour, Tabasco and mustard. Gradually add the milk, stirring constantly. When the sauce is smooth, add cheese and stir until melted. Pour into a greased baking dish that will accommodate 6 eggs.

Break eggs into the sauce and they will form a pocket. Sprinkle top with paprika. Bake at 350° for 20 minutes, or until yolks are set and sauce is bubbly. Serve on English muffins. Yield: 3 to 6 servings.

Also place a thin slice of ham on the muffin and then top with the eggs Mornay. Serve with fruit or melon to make a delicious brunch that is very little trouble.

Marlene Van Lent
BED & BREAKFAST OF NEBRASKA

Frittata

"A linen-lined basket of delights and complimentary wine greet each guest's evening arrival. The following morning a cheery breakfast is served in guest's room, the backyard deck or the dining room. This crustless quiche is one of our favorite entrees."

> 2 pounds Swiss chard, spinach, broccoli, or 4 cups diced green onion
> 4 tablespoons butter
> 1 large onion, sliced (omit if using green onion)
> 2 cloves garlic, crushed
> 1/2 teaspoon crushed basil
> 1/2 teaspoon crushed oregano
> 1/2 teaspoon crushed thyme
> 12 eggs
> Salt and pepper to taste
> 1/2 cup heavy cream or sour cream
> 2 cups shredded Swiss cheese
> 1 cup grated Parmesan cheese

Preheat oven to 350°. If using greens, wash and drain. Saute onion and garlic in butter in a large skillet until transparent. Add greens and heat approximately 3 minutes. Remove from fire and add basil, oregano and thyme.

Beat eggs lightly with salt, pepper and cream. Add 1½ cups Swiss and 1/2 cup Parmesan cheeses. Mix in sauteed greens. Pour into a greased 10-inch quiche dish.* Bake for 20 to 30 minutes.

Remove from oven and sprinkle remaining Swiss and Parmesan cheeses over top. Return to oven and cook 1 minute longer to melt cheese and brown top. Cool slightly. Yield: 8 to 10 servings.

*Can be prepared ahead to this point and refrigerated until baking.

Mary Cramer, Host
"THE BRIGGS HOUSE"
SACRAMENTO INNKEEPERS, CALIFORNIA

Ham Souffle

> 3 cups cubed French bread
> 3 cups cubed ham
> 1/2 pound Cheddar cheese, cubed
> 3 tablespoons melted butter
> 1 tablespoon dry mustard
> 3 tablespoons flour
> 3 cups milk
> 4 eggs

Layer half of the bread, ham and cheese in a greased 9- by 13-inch baking dish. Sprinkle with half of the butter, mustard and flour. Repeat. Beat together milk and eggs. Pour over layered mixture. Cover and refrigerate overnight. Preheat oven to 350° and bake, uncovered, for 1 hour. Yield: 8 servings.

Maryann Kudalis

BED & BREAKFAST UPPER MIDWEST, MINNESOTA

■ Ham it up with a layer of sliced, sauteed, fresh mushrooms. You'll need approximately 1/2 pound.

Baking a few minutes longer and allowing to set for 10 minutes before cutting into small squares, gives you a nice hot appetizer.

Huevos Rancheros

From north-of-the-border comes this Tex-Mex ranch-style entree that's delicious at breakfast, brunch or supper. As a spicy twist, the chef suggests using chopped green chilies, replacing the chili sauce, and trying Colby or Monterey Jack cheese. Serve with an avocado salad topped with a sweet and sour dressing.

1/2 cup minced onion
1 cup finely chopped green pepper
2 tablespoons vegetable oil
1 cup chili sauce*
1 can (8 ounces) tomato sauce
2 tablespoons lemon juice
1 teaspoon Worcestershire sauce
1/2 teaspoon chili powder
6 tortillas
1/4 cup vegetable oil
6 eggs
2 tablespoons butter
1/2 cup grated Cheddar cheese
6 green peppers, cleaned and sliced into thin rings

To prepare sauce: Saute onion and green pepper in 2 tablespoons oil until tender. Add chili and tomato sauces, lemon juice, Worcestershire sauce and chili powder. Bring to a boil, reduce heat and simmer 15 minutes, stirring occasionally.

While sauce is simmering, fry tortillas one at a time in 1/4 cup vegetable oil until limp, but not crisp. Drain on paper towels. Fry eggs in butter, just until firm.

To assemble: Spoon some sauce onto each tortilla. Top with an egg and more sauce. Sprinkle with cheese and garnish with green pepper rings. Yield: about 6 servings, depending on appetites.

Peg Marshall

BED AND BREAKFAST OF LOS ANGELES, CALIFORNIA

■ *Mexican chili sauce is available in cans in most markets.

Ole Potato Scramble

1/2 pound bulk sausage
1/2 medium onion, minced
1/2 small green pepper, chopped
2 medium potatoes (washed well or peeled), chopped
1/4 teaspoon, oregano
4 eggs, beaten
1/2 cup grated cheese

Brown and drain sausage. Discard drippings. Return sausage to skillet. Add onion, pepper, potatoes, oregano, eggs and cheese. Work mixture with a wooden spoon or spatula until eggs are set to desired firmness. Yield: 4 servings.

Kay Cameron
OZARK MOUNTAIN COUNTRY
BED & BREAKFAST SERVICE, MISSOURI

Joanna's Strata

3/4 pound bulk pork sausage, crumbled, cooked and drained
White bread slices, 5 or more to fit, crusts removed
Butter
3/4 pound sharp cheese, grated
4 eggs, beaten
2 cups milk
1/2 teaspoon salt
1/2 teaspoon dry mustard
1/2 teaspoon pepper
1 can (4 ounces) chopped green chilies
1 tomato, sliced

Keep bread whole or cut in half to fit casserole size. Butter both sides of bread slices and place half in casserole. Cover bread with half of cheese and then sprinkle with sausage. Add remaining bread and top with remaining cheese.

In a medium bowl, combine eggs, milk, salt, mustard and pepper. Pour over casserole. Let stand several hours, or cover and refrigerate overnight. Preheat oven to 350°. Bake covered for 50 minutes.

Remove from oven and spread chilies over casserole. Top with tomato slices. Return to oven and bake, uncovered, for an additional 10 minutes, or until set. Yield: 5 to 6 servings.

This recipe adapts easily to individual casserole servings and bakes in approximately 30 minutes.

Roberta Rosen and Rhonda Robins
HOME SUITE HOMES, CALIFORNIA

Late Drifters' Breakfast Casserole

"This recipe has drawn many compliments and some requests for copies. Breakfast tastes best when it is eaten as soon as it is cooked. However, when guests drift in late or separately to the table, it is nice to have an entree that loses nothing by waiting in a warming oven."

          2 cups plain croutons* or diced toast
          1 cup shredded Cheddar cheese
          4 eggs, beaten
          2 cups milk
          1/2 teaspoon salt
          1/2 teaspoon prepared mustard
          1/8 teaspoon onion powder
          Dash pepper
          4 strips bacon, cooked, drained and crumbled

Preheat oven to 325°. Grease an 11- by 7- by 2-inch baking dish. Combine croutons and cheese; spread in dish. In medium-size bowl, mix together eggs, milk, salt, mustard, onion powder and pepper. Pour over crouton mixture; sprinkle with bacon. Bake for 55 to 60 minutes, or until set. Yield: 6 to 8 servings.

                    Evelyn and Ed Hanlon, Hosts
                    BED AND BREAKFAST ASSOCIATES
                    BAY COLONY, LTD., MASSACHUSETTS

■ *Herb-seasoned or garlic and cheese croutons may be substituted,

Make-Ahead Breakfast

2 cups soft bread cubes from white bread, crusts removed
1 cup milk
8 eggs
4 tablespoons butter
Salt and pepper to taste
1/2 teaspoon seasoned salt
1/2 pound Swiss or Cheddar cheese, grated
1/2 cup bread crumbs
8 strips bacon, cooked, drained and crumbled

Soak bread cubes in milk and set aside. Scramble eggs VERY LIGHTLY in 2 tablespoons butter. Add soaked bread cubes; stir to combine and season with salt and pepper.

Turn into a greased 1½-quart casserole and sprinkle with seasoned salt. Top with grated cheese. Brown bread crumbs in remaining 2 tablespoons butter, add bacon and sprinkle over top. Casserole may be covered and stored in refrigerator overnight before baking, or baked immediately in a preheated 400° oven for 15 minutes, or until warmed through. Yield: 6 servings.

Judy Bowman, Host
"RED HILL FARM"
NUTMEG BED & BREAKFAST, CONNECTICUT

Margaret's Artichoke Quiche

"My guests' happiness is most important, and I take pride in providing 'western hospitality remembered,' getting their days off to an exhilarating start with this filling and delicious breakfast."

1 jar (16 ounces) marinated artichoke hearts
1/2 cup finely chopped onion
1 clove garlic, minced
4 eggs, slightly beaten
1/4 cup finely crushed dry bread crumbs
1/2 teaspoon salt
1/4 teaspoon pepper
1/4 teaspoon crushed oregano
Dash of Tabasco
3 tablespoons coarsely chopped pimiento
1/2 pound sharp Cheddar cheese, grated
2 tablespoons minced parsley

Preheat oven to 325°. Drain artichoke hearts, reserving 2 tablespoons liquid. Place reserved liquid in a frying pan; saute onion and garlic in liquid. In large bowl, combine eggs, crumbs, salt, pepper, oregano and Tabasco.

Quarter artichoke hearts. Stir pimiento, cheese and artichoke hearts into egg mixture. Add onion mixture. Stir to combine. Turn into a well-greased 7- by 11-inch baking dish. Sprinkle with parsley. Bake for 30 minutes or until set. Cool and cut into squares. Yield: 6 to 8 servings.

"I also serve this for hors d'oeuvres, warmed and cut into 1-inch squares."

Bessie Lipinski
BED AND BREAKFAST IN ARIZONA

■ Grate and freeze any leftover bits of cheese to use with eggs or as toppings.

Omelet Duvall

2 eggs
1 teaspoon water
1/2 cup cottage cheese
1/4 cup pineapple chunks, drained
Salt to taste
2 tablespoons butter
Orange slice

Whip eggs with water. In small bowl combine cottage cheese, pineapple and salt; set aside. Melt butter in an omelet pan until lightly browned. Add egg mixture and cook until set. Place cottage cheese mixture on one-half of omelet; fold over to cover filling. Flip pan and cook until firm. Garnish with orange slice. Yield: 1 serving.

Chopped chives, onion or green pepper, berries, seedless grapefruit slices or grapes may be substituted for pineapple. An electric omelet pan may also be used.

Dale Duvall
"THE QUIET RESORTS," DELAWARE

■ For sweet berry omelet, omit pineapple chunks, and add 1 teaspoon sugar to egg mixture. Toss 1 cup sliced or whole berries with 1 tablespoon sugar in bowl. Spoon onto one-half of omelet just before serving. Fold omelet and sprinkle with confectioners' sugar.

Scallion And Cheese Quiche

■ From a "self-confessed non-cook" host comes this tempting recipe, which is delicious served either piping hot or chilled.

> 1 9-inch basic shortcrust pie crust*
> 2 tablespoons butter
> 1/2 cup minced scallions
> Pinch of brewer's yeast
> 6 to 8 ounces Swiss or Gruyere cheese, cubed
> 3 eggs, beaten
> 1½ cups heavy cream
> 1/2 teaspoon nutmeg
> Salt and pepper to taste

Preheat oven to 450°. Melt butter in small saucepan and saute scallions. Sprinkle yeast over scallions; spread mixture in pie crust. Arrange cheese cubes over scallions. Blend eggs, cream and nutmeg in a blender. Add salt and pepper to taste. Pour into pie crust. Bake for 15 minutes; reduce heat to 350° and bake an additional 15 to 20 minutes. Let stand 10 minutes before cutting. Yield: 6 to 8 servings.

Kathryn Proud, Host
NEW ORLEANS BED & BREAKFAST, LOUISIANA

*See page 157.

Scrambled Eggs With Mushroom Sauce

This recipe has all the components of a great guest breakfast . . . FAST, EASY and GOURMET! Add fresh melon and English muffins and you have an attractive and satisfying breakfast.

> 2 teaspoons butter
> 6 eggs
> 6 tablespoons milk, cream or water*
> 2 ounces grated Cheddar cheese
> *Sauce:*
> 1 can (10¾ ounces) cream of mushroom soup
> 1 can (4 ounces) sliced mushrooms
> 1/4 cup dry sherry

To scramble the eggs, melt butter in skillet over medium heat. Break eggs into a bowl, add milk and mix with fork or whisk. Pour eggs into skillet and stir as mixture begins to set. Scrambled eggs should be large and fluffy.*

Place half of the eggs in each of 2 greased individual casserole dishes (or 1 1-quart casserole). Sprinkle each with half of the cheese. Add another layer of eggs and remaining cheese.

Prepare sauce by mixing soup, mushrooms and sherry in a small saucepan. Stir and heat through.

Spoon 3 to 4 tablespoons of sauce over the top of each casserole. Bake at 350° just until heated and cheese melts. Yield: 2 servings.

Serve garnished with parsley.

*Water used for scrambled eggs makes them fluffier.

EVELOS BED & BREAKFAST, MINNESOTA

■ Extra sauce will keep in refrigerator for 1 week. Reheat in microwave or stove top. Try it over poached eggs.

Seaview Quiche

"We are a Bed and Breakfast host family. Our upstairs is one large bedroom with a king-sized canopy bed, lots of books, a rocking chair and a fireplace. I try to carry out a romantic theme for our guests. Some of them like a tray in their room; others go to our sunny kitchen or patio for more 'seaview.' Wherever they are, I like to serve this quiche with sliced oranges on my best china, with linen napkins. So easy, and so pretty."

    1 cup crabmeat, chopped cooked shrimp or flaked cooked salmon
    1 tablespoon minced green onion
    1/2 cup mayonnaise
    4 teaspoons flour
    1 whole egg
    3 egg yolks
    1/2 cup milk
    8 ounces grated Swiss cheese
    1 10-inch pie shell, baked

Preheat oven to 350°. Combine crabmeat, onion, mayonnaise, flour, egg and yolks, milk and cheese. Mix well and spoon into pie shell. Bake for 45 minutes. Yield: 6 to 8 servings.

Patsy Graziani, Host
"SEAVIEW OF CARPINTERIA"
BED AND BREAKFAST - WEST COAST, CALIFORNIA

Tahoe Brunch

■ Lynn helps you get a head start with this recipe that **must be** prepared 12 hours in advance!

1½ pounds mild Italian sausage
1/2 pound mushrooms, cleaned and sliced
2 cups thinly sliced onion
1/2 cup butter
Salt and pepper to taste
12 slices bread, buttered
1 pound Cheddar cheese, grated
5 eggs
2½ cups milk
3 teaspoons Dijon mustard
1 teaspoon dry mustard
1 teaspoon nutmeg
1 teaspoon salt
1/8 teaspoon pepper
Minced parsley

Cook sausage. Drain and cut into bite-size pieces. Set aside. Brown mushrooms and onions in butter. Season with salt and pepper. In a greased 11- by 13-inch baking dish, layer half of the bread, half of the mushroom mix, half of the sausage and half of the cheese. Repeat. In blender combine eggs, milk, Dijon and dry mustards, nutmeg, salt and pepper. Pour mixture over layers, cover and refrigerate overnight. Preheat oven to 350° and bake, uncovered, for 1 hour. Sprinkle with parsley. Yield: 6 to 8 servings.

Serve with fruit salad and crusty bread.

Lynn Morgan
California Bed and Breakfast
Inn Service, California

PANCAKES, WAFFLES, DOUGHNUTS AND FRENCH TOAST

Traditionally served on weekends, these morning specials provide an expansive variety to the ordinary with the addition of toppings, sauces and fillings.

Guests enjoy the excitement of an eye-popping pancake emerging from the oven, as well as one flipping on the griddle. The regional surprises lurking between the grids of the waffle iron are anxiously awaited, also. In concert with the above are finger sweets "for dunking" into a cup of coffee or tea

Rod and Pearl Thurlow raise nearly everything they need on their farm. Even if you can't bring the eggs in from your backyard, Pearl's prize-winning homemade "mix" offers old-fashioned flavor from the pantry. When packaged and wrapped nicely, it makes a welcomed gift.

Your weekday travelers will savor these habitual end-of-the-week indulgences. Sandwiched with unusual stuffings, pancakes, waffles and French toast gain instant celebrity at the table any day of the week— any hour of the day.

Bunkhouse Deluxe French Toast

2 slices sourdough bread
Cream cheese
Chopped pecans
Egg/milk coating mixture
1 teaspoon butter
Apricot or plum jam

Spread a mixture of cream cheese and nuts, 1/4 to 1/2-inch thick, between slices of bread. Dip bread into egg/milk mixture, coating both sides. Melt butter in a skillet and saute bread, turning once. Warm jam in separate pan.

Serve French toast with several slices of Canadian bacon. Serve warmed jam from small pitcher on the side. Yield: 1 serving.

THE BUNKHOUSE, WYOMING

Double-Dip French Toast

3 eggs
2/3 cup milk
1/4 teaspoon salt
6 slices French bread
9 strips bacon, cooked and drained

Preheat greased iron griddle to proper setting. Beat eggs, milk and salt together. Dip bread slices into milk mixture, coating both sides. Saute slices on griddle until light golden brown on both sides.

Remove and dip bread slices into milk mixture again; then return them to griddle and continue to brown both sides. You may need to grease the griddle again between brownings.

For each serving, top one piece of French toast with 3 strips of bacon and cover with second piece of toast. Spread with butter and serve with a choice of syrups, honey or jellies. Yield: 3 servings.

Ruth Sharf, Host
BED & BREAKFAST OF PHILADELPHIA, PENNSYLVANIA

■ For crunchy French toast, dip bread slices in batter and then in finely crushed corn flakes, coating both sides. Fry on hot griddle, turning once.

French Toast Gloria

■ This French toast should be served hot, topped with Gloria's Orange Syrup (page 108).

1 unsliced loaf stale bread, French, brioche or cinnamon
2 eggs
2 cups milk
4 tablespoons sugar
1/4 teaspoon salt
Butter

Preheat griddle. Trim crust from bread, if desired. Slice loaf vertically into 1/2-inch slices. In small bowl beat eggs slightly. Stir in milk, sugar and salt.

Dip each side of bread into egg mixture. On hot, buttered griddle saute slices, turning once as each side becomes golden brown. Repeat until all bread is used. Yield: 4 servings.

Gloria Lyon, Host
"AMERICAN FAMILY INN"
BED & BREAKFAST SAN FRANCISCO, CALIFORNIA

Orange-Honey French Toast

2 eggs, slightly beaten
1/2 to 1 teaspoon orange-flavored instant breakfast drink powder
1/4 cup honey
1/4 teaspoon salt
6 slices bread

Beat together eggs, drink powder, honey and salt. Grease and preheat griddle. Dip bread slices into batter mixture and fry until golden brown, turning once. Yield: 3 servings.

Kay Cameron
Ozark Mountain Country
Bed & Breakfast Service, Missouri

■ These are nice dusted with powdered sugar, and served with an assortment of syrups or jellies from which guests can choose.

AEBLESKIVERS

■ Aebleskivers are Danish pancake balls cooked in a cast iron Aebleskiver pan with hemispherical wells which produce a round raised pancake about half the size of a golf ball.

There are two types of Aebleskiver pans. The one for gas ranges has rounded wells on the bottom and a skirt around the sides of the pan that sits on the burner trivet and captures the gas heat. The pan for electric ranges has no skirt and the bottom of the wells are flat for good contact with the electric element.

Aebleskivers Alma

4 cups flour
1 tablespoon sugar
1 teaspoon salt
1 teaspoon ground cardamon*
3 tablespoons baking powder
4 eggs, separated
3 cups milk
1/2 cup beer
Juice and grated rind of 1/2 lemon
1/4 cup oil
1/4 cup butter
Confectioners' sugar

Sift, then re-sift flour, sugar, salt, cardamon and baking powder into a large mixing bowl. Lightly beat egg yolks, stir milk into yolks, add to dry ingredients and mix well. Add beer, lemon juice and rind and mix well. Beat egg whites until stiff, but not dry, and fold into the batter.

Combine oil and butter in small heavy pot and heat until butter is melted. Heat Aebleskiver pan to 375°. Using a pastry brush, liberally oil each well with about 1 teaspoon of the mixture. Fill each well level with batter. Using a metal skewer or knitting needle, spear each Aebleskiver in turn from the middle toward the edge and rotate upwards a half turn.

This turns the browned portion of the Aebleskiver up out of the well and allows uncooked batter to form another portion of the ball. Turn again in like fashion. The last turn should position the small remaining opening in the ball at the bottom of the well.

Total cooking time is about 6 to 8 minutes. The last turn must be made while some batter is still uncooked to form a complete sphere. The Aebleskivers may be cooked further to desired brown crust by rotating periodically in the well.

To keep Aebleskivers hot, take from pan and place in wooden bowl and put into a slow 200° oven until enough are made for serving. Dust with confectioners' sugar before serving.

The traditional Danish way to serve Aebleskivers is with sausage links, fresh applesauce and fresh raspberry sauce.† Yield: 25 to 30 pancake balls.

Leftover Aebleskivers can be frozen. To reheat, thaw very slowly in toaster oven at lowest possible setting until heated through. This leaves the outer crust crisp and the center soft.

*Freshly ground cardamon makes an extraordinary difference in the taste and aroma of the Aebleskivers. Since whole cardamon is extremely expensive, an acceptable improvement can be obtained by shelling and grinding the seeds of one cardamon with a mortar and pestle and adding to packaged ground cardamon.

Jean Brown
BED & BREAKFAST INTERNATIONAL, CALIFORNIA

■ †See recipe for Raspberry Sauce this chapter, page 108.

Banana Pancakes

2 eggs
1 cup milk
2 bananas, peeled and quartered
1 cup biscuit mix
1 cup whole wheat and honey pancake mix*

Blend eggs, milk and bananas in blender on high, until smooth. Set aside 1/2 of mixture in bowl. Add 1/2 of biscuit mix and 1/2 of pancake mix to blender, blending until well moistened. Add remaining mixture and continue blending until well combined. (Add more milk if thinner pancake is desired.) For each pancake pour 1/4 cup batter onto a hot, buttered griddle. Cook until golden brown, turning once. Yield: Twenty 4-inch cakes.

Serve with luscious, hot maple or raspberry syrup.

Sylva Jones
WESTERN BED & BREAKFAST HOSTS, MONTANA

■ *Can substitute any pancake mix sweetened with 1/4 cup honey. Great idea for those over-ripe bananas that no one will eat.

Breezemere Blueberry Pancakes

"Breezemere Farm is known for its natural foods. No synthetics or preservatives are used. Vegetables are organically grown, eggs laid by farm hens, butter freshly churned and breads hearth-baked."

Blueberries are a Maine classic, and these pancakes are a Breezemere specialty!

2 cups flour
1/4 cup sugar
4 teaspoons baking powder
1 teaspoon salt
2 eggs
2 cups milk
1 teaspoon vanilla
1/4 cup vegetable oil
3 cups fresh blueberries,* cleaned and picked over
Butter

In a large bowl, sift together flour, sugar, baking powder and salt. Crack eggs into center and stir until blended. In a small bowl blend milk, vanilla and oil with a whisk. Pour into dry mixture, stirring only enough to moisten all the flour. NEVER BEAT BATTER. Cook on a hot, greased griddle, turning once when bottom is golden brown. Yield: Twenty 4-inch pancakes.

Joan Lippke
"BREEZEMERE FARM," MAINE

■ *Frozen blueberries do fine when freshly picked blueberries are unavailable. When freezing fresh blueberries, do not wash after picking. Spread on a cookie sheet, put in freezer. When frozen, put in plastic freezer bags and store in freezer.

Country Apple Fritters

1 cup flour
1 teaspoon baking powder
1 teaspoon salt
2 eggs
1/2 cup milk
1 teaspoon vegetable oil
3 cups cubed apples,* unpared
Vegetable oil for frying

Combine flour, baking powder, salt, eggs, milk and 1 teaspoon oil. Beat until batter is smooth. Fold in apples. Heat vegetable oil in a 10-inch skillet to 375°. Drop apple batter by tablespoonfuls into pan. Turn once to brown on both sides. Remove with slotted spoon, and drain on paper towels.†. Yield: 18 fritters.

Veronica LaRoy, Host
BETSY ROSS BED & BREAKFAST, MICHIGAN

■ *Or use other cubed fruit such as pears or peaches.
†Sprinkle with granulated sugar and cinnamon while warm.
We suggest serving with pitchers of honey and warm maple syrup.

Crispy Pancakes

■ While New York City has not gone down as a hearty breakfast center, this host can whip up a meaningful and exciting experience, especially for young guests, with the following pancakes. These pancakes hold their shape in the skillet, allowing puppy dogs, tepees and initials to magically appear on a child's plate.

    1½ cups flour
    3 teaspoons baking powder
    1/2 teaspoon salt
    1 cup milk
    2 eggs
    2 tablespoons butter

Combine flour, baking powder, salt, milk and eggs in a pitcher. Stir well. To make a thinner pancake, add more milk. Melt butter in a hot skillet. Drizzle batter from a spoon to create desired design. Cook until golden brown. Yield: 3 cups.

Mary McAulay
URBAN VENTURES, NEW YORK

■ Children also love "crispy pancakes" wrapped around cooked hot dogs or sausage links and served with Los Gatos sunshine riser and toasted cinnamon milk sticks. (See pages 15 and 61.)

Dutch Babies

■ Pamper your Dutch Babies with nutmeg, cinnamon, allspice, cloves, powdered or brown sugar, warm syrups, lemon juice, warm or fresh fruits, creamed ham or dried beef. Guests enjoy the personal touch of individual ramekins. Fill each ramekin about 1/4 full, turn on your oven light and watch the excitement.

Pan Size:	2-3 quart	3-4 quart	4-4½ quart	4½-5 quart
Serves:	4	6	8	10
Butter:	1/4 cup	1/3 cup	1/2 cup	1/2 cup
Eggs:	3	4	5	6
Milk:	3/4 cup	1 cup	1¼ cups	1½ cups
Flour:	3/4 cup	1 cup	1¼ cups	1½ cups

Place butter in cast iron skillet or oven pottery in the size you have chosen. Place pan in a 425° oven.

In blender place eggs and whirl at high speed for 1 minute. Gradually pour in milk, then gradually add flour. Continue whirling for 30 seconds. Remove pan from oven and pour batter into hot pan. Return to oven and bake about 20 to 25 minutes, until puffy and well browned.

Jack Evans and Pamela Evans
"THE COACH HOUSE INN," OREGON

Freezer Pancake Batter

5 eggs
4 teaspoons baking powder
4 tablespoons sugar
4 tablespoons vegetable oil
2 teaspoons vanilla
1 teaspoon salt
4 cups sifted flour

In a large mixing bowl, mix eggs, baking powder, sugar, oil, vanilla, salt and flour with electric mixer. Pour into 1/2-gallon milk cartons and freeze.

When ready to use, thaw and beat well. Pour batter into hot, greased skillet in amounts to produce pancakes slightly thicker than crepes. Yield: About forty-eight 6-inch pancakes.

Tom Atkinson, Host
"ANCHOR HILL RANCH"
OZARK MT. COUNTRY B&B, MISSOURI

Funnel Cake

■ Funnel Cake is a traditional food of the Amish; however, this recipe came to us from Tennessee. There are "walk-away" Funnel Cake stalls in San Francisco, so, you might call it a "national favorite."

The fun in Funnel Cake is in the making, and with proper supervision and caution about the hot oil, children can put their artistic talents to work pouring whimsical designs.

> 1 ⅓ cups flour, sifted
> 2 tablespoons sugar
> 1/4 teaspoon salt
> 3/4 tablespoons baking powder
> 2/3 cup milk
> 1 egg, beaten
> Vegetable oil
> Confectioners' sugar or cinnamon sugar (optional)

Sift flour, sugar, salt and baking powder together. Mix milk and egg together. Beat egg mixture into dry ingredients until batter is smooth. Heat 3/4 inch of oil in a skillet to 375°. Using a funnel,* holding finger over bottom while filling, drizzle batter from funnel into skillet in a free-form continual spiral or web design about 4 or 5 inches in diameter, being careful not to fill in entire area of design.

Fry until golden brown, turning once with tongs. Drain on paper toweling. Dip in confectioners' sugar or cinnamon sugar. Serve immediately. Yield: 12 to 14.

Betty Cordellos
NASHVILLE BED & BREAKFAST, TENNESSEE

■ *A pitcher or condiment-type container with squeeze top is easier to use.

Drizzle funnel cakes with maple syrup; remember to serve with a knife and fork, as they will be sticky.

Klejner

3 eggs
3/4 cup sugar
Grated rind of 1 lemon
2/3 cup butter
3 tablespoons cream
3¾ cups flour
Vegetable oil
Confectioners' sugar

In a large bowl, cream eggs and sugar together until lemon colored. Stir in grated lemon rind and butter. Add cream and flour and work into a smooth dough with hands. Roll dough 1/4 inch thick, and cut into strips 4 inches long by 1 inch wide. Slant ends and make a slit in center of each strip. Put one end through slit to form a knot. Heat 3 inches of oil in skillet, and fry cookies until light brown. Drain on paper toweling, and sprinkle with confectioners' sugar. Stores well in tightly covered container. Yield: About 3 dozen.

Bente Krarup, Host
BED & BREAKFAST CO., FLORIDA

Pearl's Pancake "Mix"

■ Rod and Pearl Thurlow live on a 160-acre farm, where most of the fresh ingredients that go into their hearty breakfasts are grown. Pearl writes:

"Our guests choose us because this is what they desire. We are not glamorous, but just what we are—a common farm couple. Through their eyes we appreciate what we have, what money cannot buy—fresh air, sunsets, quiet, noises of nature, space, independence, all freedom that we allow ourselves, a natural family life on the farm . . . and the best of food from nature. We are nearly self-sustaining, except for electricity, coffee and orange juice."

6 cups whole wheat or white flour
4 cups corn meal
2 cups oatmeal
1/4 cup baking powder
2 tablespoons baking soda
1/4 cup salt
1/2 cup sugar

Combine flour, corn meal, oatmeal, baking powder, soda, salt and sugar. Blend well. Store in an air-tight container until ready to use. Yield: 12 cups "mix."

To use:
1 large apple, cored and coarsely chopped
2 eggs
1 cup milk
2 tablespoons oil
1 cup "mix," or more

Combine apple, eggs, milk and oil in blender and mix well. Add enough "mix" to reach desired consistency, approximately 1 cup. Grease and preheat griddle. Drop batter by tablespoonfuls onto griddle, and cook until golden brown, flipping once. Yield: about eight 4-inch cakes.

Pearl Thurlow
BED 'N' BREAKFAST ON OUR FARM, KANSAS

Potato Pancakes

■ According to this host, rendered chicken fat is the "secret ingredient" to perfection of taste in these pancakes.

5 medium potatoes, washed, peeled and quartered
1/4 teaspoon salt
1 teaspoon rendered chicken fat
1 tablespoon matzo meal
1 large onion, chopped
Safflower oil

Pulverize potatoes in blender. Add salt, chicken fat, matzo meal and onion. Grease hot skillet with safflower oil. Drop batter by spoonfuls onto hot skillet, cooking until crispy brown crust forms, turning once. Yield: 6 generous servings.

Serve with homemade applesauce or sour cream.

Tiba Willner
BED & BREAKFAST IN OJAI, CALIFORNIA

Sourdough Pancakes

1 cup sourdough starter*
2 cups flour
2 cups milk
1 teaspoon salt
2 teaspoons baking soda
2 eggs
3 tablespoons shortening, melted
2 tablespoons sugar

Mix starter, flour, milk and salt in a 3-quart bowl; cover and let stand overnight in a warm place.

In the morning, take 1 cup of batter and return to the starter. To remaining batter add baking soda, eggs, shortening and sugar. Beat well. Drop onto lightly greased griddle (about 3 tablespoons per pancake) turning when bubbles start to appear and bottoms are golden brown.

*For Sourdough Starter recipe, see Index.

Marlene Van Lent
BED & BREAKFAST OF NEBRASKA

Swedish Plättar Cakes

Memories of yesteryear from San Francisco—Grandma's plättar; the aroma of pancakes warming on a towel-covered baking sheet in a slow oven; pitchers of warmed orange syrup, honey and lingonberry sauces—and these plättar cakes.

3 eggs
1¼ cups milk
3/4 cup flour, sifted
1 tablespoon sugar
1/2 teaspoon salt
Butter

In a large mixing bowl, beat eggs until thick and lemon colored. Stir in milk. Sift together dry ingredients and add to egg and milk mixture, mixing until smooth. (Batter will be thin.) Drop ONE TABLESPOON of batter onto moderately hot, buttered plättar.* Tilt to spread batter evenly to edges, forming a thin, crepe-like pancake. Turn once to brown evenly. Yield: 3½ dozen 3-inch cakes.

Gloria Lyon, Host
"AMERICAN FAMILY INN"
BED & BREAKFAST SAN FRANCISCO, CALIFORNIA

*Available in specialty shops or you can use a regular griddle.

■ Arie, a Bed & Breakfast International host from California, makes 10-inch cakes, stacks 6 to 8 pancakes on a serving plate, spreads butter between them, and cuts them into pie-shaped wedges. Jelly or maple syrup is served for topping. Bowls of cinnamon sugar, whipped cream and crushed berries on the table allow guests to top with their own choices. For a great dessert, spread almond paste between stacked pancakes, top with whipped cream and sprinkle with sliced almonds.

Swiss Enchiladas Crepes

Crepes:
2 eggs
2 egg yolks
1 teaspoon salt
1 cup flour
1 cup beer
2 tablespoons sour cream
1 tablespoon melted butter

Filling:
2 onions, chopped
2 tablespoons oil
2 cloves garlic, minced
1 can (30 ounces) tomato sauce or puree (fresh is wonderful)
4 cans (3 ounces each) chopped green chilies
4 cups cooked chicken (2 or 3 breasts)
1 teaspoon salt
1 pound Jack cheese, shredded
4 chicken bouillon cubes
2 cups half-and-half or light cream

Combine ingredients for crepes in blender jar; blend for about 1 minute. Scrape down sides with rubber spatula and blend for another 15 seconds or until smooth. Refrigerate at least 1 hour before cooking according to instructions with any type crepe pan (this is the method I use, but any way is possible with this recipe). Yield: 22 to 35 crepes, depending on pan size.

For filling, saute onion in oil in large saucepan until soft. Add garlic, tomato sauce, chilies, chicken and salt. Simmer 10 minutes (can be stored in airtight container overnight at this point).

Fill crepes in rolled fashion and place in casserole dish. Combine cheese, bouillon and cream. Pour over filled crepes. Bake at 350° for 20 to 30 minutes.

"We serve this with either corn pudding or sweet potato Saratoga chips and garnish with avocado slices."

Nan Hawkins
BARNARD-GOOD HOUSE OF CAPE MAY, NEW JERSEY

Tia's Buttermilk Pancakes

1/2 teaspoon baking soda
1 cup buttermilk*
1½ cups flour
1 teaspoon baking powder
1 teaspoon sugar
1 teaspoon salt
3 eggs, separated
3 to 4 tablespoons butter, melted
1 cup milk

Dissolve baking soda in the buttermilk. Sift flour, baking powder, sugar and salt together. Beat egg yolks and melted butter into dry ingredients. Add buttermilk and milk; stir to blend. Beat egg whites stiff and fold in. Drop by soupspoonfuls onto hot griddle, flipping once when evenly browned. Yield: 4 to 6 servings of silver dollar-size pancakes.

*For making your own buttermilk or sour milk, combine 1 teaspoon lemon juice plus milk to measure 1 cup. Let stand 5 minutes before using.

Rick Madden
BED & BREAKFAST COLORADO

Best Waffles

1¾ cups flour
3 teaspoons baking powder
1/2 teaspoon salt
3 eggs, separated
1¾ cups milk
1/2 cup liquid shortening

In medium bowl, combine flour, baking powder and salt; set aside. Beat egg yolks, then beat in milk and shortening. Add to dry ingredients, mixing lightly. Beat egg whites and gently fold into batter. Pour onto pre-heated waffle iron and bake until golden brown. Yield: About 1 dozen.

Bob Williams, Chef
GRANDMA'S BED & BREAKFAST, CALIFORNIA

French Toast Waffles

1 egg, beaten
1/4 cup milk
2 tablespoons melted butter
1/8 teaspoon salt
4 slices bread, halved diagonally

Preheat waffle iron. Combine egg, milk, butter and salt in small dish. Dip bread slices into egg mixture, turning to coat each side. Bake in greased* waffle iron until golden brown, approximately 4 minutes. Yield: 2 servings.

*If using waffle iron with non-stick surface, do not grease. Quantities can be increased to accommodate larger crowds.

GATEWAY B AND B, MISSOURI

Nutty Raisin Bran Waffles

1½ cups flour
4 teaspoons baking powder
3/4 teaspoon salt
1½ tablespoons sugar
2 cups cereal (bran)
3 eggs
2¼ cups milk
1/3 cup vegetable oil
1/2 cup finely chopped pecans
3/4 cup raisins

Mix flour, baking powder, salt, sugar and cereal together in a medium-size bowl and set aside. Beat together eggs, milk and vegetable oil in another bowl. Add liquid to dry ingredients and beat until smooth. Fold in pecans and raisins. Bake on preheated waffle iron until golden. Yield: 1 dozen.

Kay Cameron
OZARK MOUNTAIN COUNTRY
BED & BREAKFAST SERVICE, MISSOURI

Vines' Old Fashioned Golden Waffles

1 cup self-rising flour
1 tablespoon sugar
2 tablespoons shortening
2 eggs, separated
Butter

Combine flour, sugar and shortening. Beat egg yolks slightly and stir into flour mixture. Beat egg whites until stiff and fold into mixture. Bake on greased waffle iron until golden. Yield: Three 4-part waffles.

Herb and Jennet Vines, Hosts
BED & BREAKFAST BIRMINGHAM, ALABAMA

■ Waffle batter keeps in the refrigerator for approximately 3 days. Store covered. Leftover waffles are delicious warmed in the toaster or toaster oven. Create a Belgian dessert by topping with ice cream and hot fudge sauce.

Elsa's German Syrup

2 cups brown sugar
1 cup light corn syrup
1/2 cup cream
1 egg

Boil brown sugar and syrup together for about 3 minutes. Beat cream and egg together, then beat into hot syrup. Yield: approximately 2 cups.

"Delicious on waffles and pancakes."

Mary Shaw
BED & BREAKFAST CHICAGO INC., ILLINOIS

Mountain Country Syrup

2 cups honey
4 tablespoons lemon juice
4 tablespoons butter

Combine honey, lemon juice and butter in small saucepan. Stir over medium heat until honey is dissolved and butter is melted. Serve warm. Yield: About 3 cups.

Store covered in refrigerator and reheat slowly, as needed.

Kay Cameron
OZARK MOUNTAIN COUNTRY
BED & BREAKFAST SERVICE, MISSOURI

Orange Syrup

"Some of our most interesting breakfast entertainment was provided by a professional magician from Atlanta. He regaled us each morning with mind-bending feats of magic. Several months after his departure there was an early morning phone call from him. 'Today is Father's Day, and I want my wife to make me the same Orange Syrup for my pancakes, as I had at your house. Could you give her the recipe over the phone?'"

■ Save your money. Gloria has the recipe right here for you.

> 1 cup sweet butter
> 1 can (6 ounces) orange juice concentrate
> 1 cup sugar

Combine butter, juice and sugar in medium saucepan. Place over low heat until butter is melted, stirring occasionally. Do not boil. Remove from heat, beat and serve warm.* Yield: 2 cups.

Store covered in refrigerator for several weeks. When reheating, heat slowly, remembering not to boil.

Gloria Lyon, Host
"American Family Inn"
Bed & Breakfast San Francisco, California

■ *To keep syrup warm for serving, place in a small chafing dish over a candle or in a double boiler simmering on stove-top.

Raspberry Sauce

> 1 package (10 ounces) frozen raspberries
> 2 teaspoons cornstarch
> 1/2 cup water

Place frozen raspberries into a heavy pot with a tight-fitting cover and put on low heat. When berries are thawed, remove cover and bring to boiling point, but do not boil. Dissolve cornstarch in water and stir 1 teaspoon of thickener at a time into the raspberries until desired consistency is obtained. The sauce should not be too thick. Serve hot. Yield: About 1 cup.

"Leftover sauces (covered with plastic) are best reheated in the microwave oven."

Jean Brown
B&B International, California

BRUNCH MAIN DISHES

These recipes are the "meat and potatoes"– "bacon and eggs" of an All-American breakfast. As the backbone or the mainstay, each recipe will stand on its own and is enhanced by selections from the other chapters in this book. Many of the dishes are interchangeable as brunch, lunch, supper or late-dinner entrees. Many are regional and traditional favorites of B&B hosts.

Asparagus Toast

■ To be in Holland during the "SPARGLE" season is a delight. Dutch asparagus is the white variety that never sees the light of day while growing, as it is kept covered with earth. The following recipe from New Hampshire can be served for breakfast, lunch or supper, using the tender green shoots grown in our country.

    1 tablespoon Dijon mustard
    2 tablespoons butter, softened
    6 slices whole wheat bread,* lightly toasted
    6 thin slices ham
    18 fresh asparagus spears, washed and cooked crisp-tender†
    4 ounces grated Mozzarella cheese
    2 tablespoons mayonnaise
    1/4 cup minced green onions
    2 tablespoons chopped pimiento
    1 tablespoon sesame seeds, toasted

Preheat broiler. Combine mustard and butter. Divide mixture evenly on toast. Top each slice with ham and three asparagus spears (you may slice asparagus diagonally before assembly for easier eating). Combine cheese, mayonnaise, onions, pimiento and sesame seeds and spread over asparagus. Place on cookie sheet and broil 5 to 6 inches from heat for 4 to 5 minutes, until cheese topping melts, and is golden brown. Yield: 6 servings.

Darrell Trapp
"Whitneys' Village Inn," New Hampshire

■ *Whole Wheat Herb Bread (See page 50) is great, too!
†Firm to the bite. This elegant rite of spring, "Asparagus Officinalis," should be cooked crisp-tender. After washing, snap off the tough ends at the tenderest point, place in a steamer basket over approximately 2 inches of boiling water. Steam, covered, 4 to 10 minutes, depending on spears' thickness.

Beef-Tomato Salsa

Not for the timid. This makes a pungent dipping sauce for breakfast cornbread or to be spooned over eggs.

> 5 pounds bone-in chuck roast, boned and cubed
> Salt and pepper to taste
> 3 tablespoons white vinegar
> Choose 2 pepper varieties from the following: New Mexico, Ancho, California, Cascabel or dried hot chilies
> 1/2 cup hot water
> 1 clove garlic
> 2 teaspoons cumin
> 1 teaspoon black pepper
> 1/2 teaspoon cinnamon
> 1/2 can (14 ounces) tomatillos, drained
>
> *Salsa:*
> 1 pound fresh ripe tomatoes, coarsely chopped
> 1 green pepper, coarsely chopped
> 1 cup diced green onion
> 1/3 cup chopped fresh coriander, or 1 teaspoon cilantro, crushed
> Salt to taste

Sprinkle meat with salt, pepper and vinegar. Refrigerate 2 to 3 hours. Discard stems of chilies, break into pieces and cover with hot water; set aside. Drain.

In blender combine garlic, cumin, pepper, cinnamon, tomatillos and drained chilies. Whirl until chilies are finely chopped.

To prepare salsa, combine tomatoes and green pepper with green onions, coriander or cilantro and salt in bowl. Chill and drain before using.

Preheat oven to 350°. Drain meat and place in 5- to 6-quart Dutch oven. Drain chilies and spread over meat. Bake covered 2½ to 3 hours, until very tender.

When ready to serve, shred meat. Serve salsa separately, to spoon over meat. Yield: 6 to 8 servings.

Sarah-Margaret Brown
NEW ORLEANS BED & BREAKFAST, LOUISIANA

■ After handling chilies, or other peppers, always wash hands with soap and water to avoid a burning sensation on your skin.

Bunk House Chili

3 pounds round steak, cut into bite-size pieces
4 tablespoons olive oil
3 pounds Italian sausage
3 cloves garlic, crushed
4 small onions, finely chopped
1 cup finely chopped celery
1 cup finely chopped green pepper
4 cans (16 ounces each) stewed tomatoes
2 jars (12 ounces each) green chili salsa
1 can (4 ounces) chopped green chilies
1/2 teaspoon cayenne pepper
1/4 teaspoon comino (cumin)
4 teaspoons chili powder
2 bay leaves
1 teaspoon oregano (Mexican, if available)
1/4 teaspoon crushed basil
1 ounce unsweetened cocoa
Salt to taste

Brown steak in oil. Add sausage; cook until browned. Drain and return to pan; mix in garlic, onion, celery and green pepper. Mash tomatoes with wooden spoon and add to pan. Add salsa, chilies, cayenne, cumin, chili powder, bay leaves, oregano, basil, cocoa and salt and cook over medium heat approximately 30 minutes. Lower temperature and simmer at least 2 hours. Discard bay leaves. Serves 12 bunk-house appetites. Or, freeze half in an air-tight container. Yield: 1½ gallons.

Suzanne, Host
BED & BREAKFAST ROCKY MOUNTAINS, COLORADO

Casserole "House Of The Stars"

1 cup medium noodles, cooked
Salt and pepper to taste
6 tablespoons grated Parmesan cheese
6 hard-boiled eggs, sliced
12 large stuffed olives, sliced
1/2 pound mushrooms, cleaned and sliced
5 tablespoons butter
3 tablespoons flour
1 cup milk
3/4 cup rich chicken stock
2 egg yolks

Grease a 2-quart casserole. Distribute noodles evenly on bottom and season with salt and pepper. Sprinkle with 4 tablespoons cheese. Arrange egg slices over cheese. Cover with olives. Saute mushrooms in 2 tablespoons butter until lightly browned. Spoon over olives. Melt remaining butter in pan. Blend in flour, and gradually whisk in milk and chicken stock until smooth. Cook over low heat, stirring constantly until thickened. Remove from heat. Stir a spoonful into egg yolks. Then beat egg yolks into sauce. Pour over casserole. Sprinkle with remaining cheese. Bake in preheated 350° oven approximately 20 minutes or until browned. Yield: 4 to 5 servings.

Richard Maloy, Host
BED & BREAKFAST OF PHILADELPHIA, PENNSYLVANIA

Cheese Puffs and Ham

Puffs:
1½ cups milk
6 tablespoons butter
3/4 teaspoon salt
Dash of pepper
1½ cups flour
6 eggs
1½ cups shredded Swiss or sharp cheese

Filling:
1/4 cup butter
1/4 cup flour
1/2 teaspoon dry mustard
1/4 teaspoon salt
Dash black and cayenne pepper
2¼ cups milk
1/2 cup shredded Swiss cheese
1/4 cup grated fresh Parmesan cheese
2 cups cooked ham (1/2 pound), chopped
2 tablespoons butter
1/2 pound mushrooms, sliced
1 tablespoon parsley

To make puffs, combine milk, butter, salt and pepper in large saucepan. Bring to a full boil over medium heat. Add flour all at once and stir until mixture leaves sides of pan and forms a ball. Remove from heat and beat in eggs, one at a time, until mixture is smooth and well blended. Beat in 1 cup cheese. Using 2 large spoons, make 12 equal mounds of dough and place 2 inches apart on a greased baking sheet. Sprinkle remaining cheese evenly over the mounds. Bake in 375° oven for 30 to 35 minutes or until puffs are well browned and crisp.

For filling, melt 1/4 cup butter in saucepan. Add the flour, mustard, salt, pepper and cayenne. Cook and stir until frothy. Add milk, cook and stir over medium-high heat until smooth and thick. Stir in cheese until melted. Combine 1 cup of sauce with chopped ham. In another skillet cook mushrooms in 2 tablespoons butter until tender. Stir mushrooms into ham mixture along with parsley. Spoon mixture into cheese puffs at serving, holding puffs warm in a chafing dish or on warming tray. Yield: 12 servings.

"This is served with either kasha or baked apple slices. It needs no garnish but poached fresh pears in cranberry juice and cinnamon stick is very nice."

Nan Hawkins
BARNARD-GOOD HOUSE OF CAPE MAY, NEW JERSEY

Corn Casserole

"Guests delight in browsing through our herb garden picking the herbs for this satisfying dish."

　　1 large onion, coarsely chopped
　　1 tablespoon butter
　　1 can (16 ounces) whole-kernel corn, drained
　　1 can (16 ounces) cream-style corn
　　2 eggs, beaten
　　1½ cups crushed saltine crackers
　　1 tablespoon prepared mustard
　　1 tablespoon minced parsley
　　1 tablespoon chopped chives
　　1 tablespoon thyme
　　1 teaspoon rosemary
　　1 teaspoon fresh sage or 1/2 teaspoon dried sage
　　1 cup milk
　　6 slices bacon or 6 sausage links, lightly fried and drained

Brown onion in butter until soft. Mix with corn, eggs, crackers, mustard, parsley, chives, thyme, rosemary, sage and milk until well combined. Pour into a buttered 13-by 9- by 2-inch ovenproof casserole dish. Arrange bacon or sausage on top. Bake, uncovered, in 350° oven 45 minutes. Yield: 4 to 6 servings.

　　"Can be prepared ahead, covered and refrigerated overnight."

"The Garrett-Drake House"
SOUTHERN COMFORT BED & BREAKFAST
RESERVATION SERVICE, LOUISIANA

Cecily's Own Crab Cakes

　　1 pound crabmeat, picked over to remove cartilage
　　1/2 cup mayonnaise
　　Dash Worcestershire sauce
　　2 eggs, beaten
　　12 single saltines, crushed
　　Butter

Combine crabmeat, mayonnaise, Worcestershire, eggs and crackers, blending well. Form into 8 patties. Saute in butter over medium to low heat, turning once, until lightly browned on both sides. Yield: 4 servings.

Cecily Sharp-Whitehill
SHARP-ADAMS, INC., MARYLAND

■ Fresh lemon circles and minced parsley are nice for garnish.

Crab/Mushroom Delights

3 strips bacon
1/4 pound fresh mushrooms, washed and sliced
1 medium onion, minced
1 cup crabmeat*
1 cup grated Swiss cheese
1/2 cup mayonnaise
6 English muffins, toasted and buttered, or 6 thick slices French bread, toasted and buttered
Cayenne
Paprika

Cut bacon into 1-inch pieces; cook until crisp and drain on paper towels, reserving bacon drippings. Saute mushrooms and onions in reserved bacon drippings until mushrooms are browned. Set aside to cool. Mix crabmeat, cheese and mayonnaise in large bowl. Fold in bacon, mushrooms and onion until blended. Pre-heat oven to 400°. Spread mixture on muffins or bread. Sprinkle with cayenne and paprika. Place on cookie sheet and bake for 10 to 15 minutes. Yield: 6 servings.

*One cup shrimp may be substituted.

Linda Moore, Anchorage guest
NEW ORLEANS BED & BREAKFAST, LOUISIANA

Florida Sukiyaki

1 medium eggplant, peeled and cubed
1/2 cup tamari or soy sauce
3 tablespoons vegetable or chicken stock
6 scallions, cut into 1½-inch pieces
1 medium onion, thickly sliced
1 cup shredded Chinese cabbage
1 can (5 ounces) bamboo shoots, drained
8 mushrooms, cleaned and halved
12 ounces thin whole wheat noodles
Crushed garlic to taste
1 teaspoon ginger
1/2 teaspoon marjoram or to taste
1/2 teaspoon tarragon or to taste
1/2 teaspoon basil or to taste
Watercress

Marinate cubed eggplant in tamari for 1 to 2 hours. Heat stock in wok or large skillet. Add scallions, onion and cabbage; simmer, covered, 2 to 3 minutes. Drain eggplant, reserving 2 teaspoons marinade. Add eggplant and reserved marinade to skillet mixture. One by one, add bamboo shoots, mushrooms and noodles. Combine garlic, ginger, marjoram, tarragon and basil. Stir into vegetables. Cover and simmer 15 to 25 minutes, or until eggplant is tender. Serve garnished with watercress. Yield: 4 to 6 servings.

Olive Grethen, Host
BED & BREAKFAST CO., FLORIDA

Fresh Pork Sausage

3 pounds pork shoulder, cubed
1/2 teaspoon cayenne pepper
3/4 teaspoon sugar
1¼ teaspoons salt
1 teaspoon freshly ground black pepper
1/4 teaspoon crushed bay leaf
1/4 teaspoon crushed thyme
3/4 teaspoon powdered sage

Grind meat and spices together with coarse blade in food chopper. Grind again with fine blade. Pack sausage in a crock and cover with wax paper. Store in coldest part of refrigerator (not longer than 5 days). As needed, shape into patties and saute. Yield: 3 pounds or approximately 36 patties of 3-inch diameter.

Olive Bree, Host

A REASONABLE ALTERNATIVE, INC.

BED & BREAKFAST ON LONG ISLAND, NEW YORK

■ Freeze patties in 1-pound packages and use as breakfast pizzas. Place a sauteed patty on an English muffin half and top with a slice of Mozzarella. Add a spoonful of tomato sauce and sprinkle with Parmesan. Broil until cheese melts. Presto, pizza!

This homemade fresh sausage can be used to make sausage rolls, sausage ring, strata or any recipe calling for fresh sausage!

General Potter's Farm's Creamed Poultry In Bread Baskets

1/2 cup butter
1/4 cup flour
2 cups milk
1/2 teaspoon salt
1/4 teaspoon white pepper
1 small onion, chopped
1 teaspoon Worcestershire sauce
1/4 cup sliced mushrooms
2 cups cooked and cubed poultry (chicken or turkey)
1/4 cup chopped red or green pepper (optional)
Bread Baskets (recipe follows)

Melt butter in saucepan. Blend in flour and cook, stirring for 3 minutes. Add milk slowly; stirring constantly until sauce thickens. Add salt, pepper, onion, Worcestershire, mushrooms and poultry; also, peppers if desired. Heat through, but do not boil. Spoon into "Bread Baskets" and serve immediately. Yield: 4 servings.

Bread Baskets

4 slices white bread, crusts removed
2 tablespoons butter, softened

With a rolling pin, flatten bread. Spread 1 side of each slice with butter. Press bread, buttered side down, into muffin tins. Bake at 350° degrees for 10 minutes. Remove from muffin tins and place each on a plate.

Bert and Freya Phillips, Hosts
"GENERAL POTTER'S FARM"
REST & REPAST, PENNSYLVANIA

■ These Bread Baskets can be made and stored in an airtight container for a short time. They can also be frozen for up to 2 months.

Gumbo Z'Herbes

"Most of our Creole and Cajun everyday foods are economical, nutritious and easy to prepare. Though when I first heard of 'Gumbo Z'Herbes,' I thought it an impossible recipe. But upon making, tasting and receiving compliments, I found it to be scrumptious."

4 cups water or stock
1 can (16 ounces) spinach
1 package (10 ounces) frozen chopped turnip greens
1 package (10 ounces) frozen chopped collard greens
1/2 medium cabbage head, finely shredded
1/3 cup minced parsley
3 tablespoons butter
3 tablespoons flour
1 pound veal stew meat, cut into 1-inch cubes
3/4 cup chopped onion
3/4 cup minced green onion with tops
1 ham hock or meaty ham bone
1 bay leaf
3/4 teaspoon salt
1/4 teaspoon basil
1/8 teaspoon allspice
1/8 teaspoon cayenne
1 can (8 ounces) oysters with liquor
1 tablespoon filé powder*

In water or stock, boil spinach, turnip greens, collards, cabbage and parsley. Reduce heat and simmer 15 minutes. Cool and blend 1 quart of this mixture in blender; set aside with unblended mixture. Melt butter in large skillet and brown flour, stirring constantly until dark brown, but not burned. Add veal and onion; brown. Stir in reserved greens, ham, bay leaf, salt, basil, allspice and cayenne; simmer covered for 2 hours, stirring occasionally. Add oysters and simmer an additional 5 minutes until heated through. Remove from heat and stir in filé. Yield: 3 quarts.

Serve over hot fluffy rice. Chicken is a great substitute for the veal.
Sarah-Margaret Brown
NEW ORLEANS BED & BREAKFAST, LOUISIANA

■ *Filé is dried sassafras leaves and is used as a thickener. Okra is often substituted for the filé.

Maltese Baked Ziti

"Maltese in origin, this recipe differs from the Italian version and has long been a favorite of both my family and my guests."

1 large onion, chopped
5 cloves garlic, minced
1 small eggplant, sliced
4 tablespoons vegetable oil (half olive oil, optional)
1 can (32 ounces) whole tomatoes, chopped and drained
1/2 teaspoon Worcestershire sauce
1 teaspoon crushed marjoram
1 teaspoon crushed oregano
3 packets beef bouillon (or 3 cubes, crushed)
Salt and pepper to taste
1 pound ground beef (or 1/2 pound ground beef and 1/2 pound ground pork)
1 pound ziti
8 eggs
3 ounces grated Parmesan cheese
1/2 pound ricotta cheese (optional)

Saute onion, garlic and eggplant in oil in a large skillet, adding more oil if necessary. tender, add tomatoes, Worcestershire, marjoram, oregano, bouillon, salt and pepper. Simmer 30 minutes. Crumble ground beef into mixture and simmer an additional 30 minutes. (Sauce should be quite thick.)

While sauce is simmering, cook ziti according to package directions, until *al dente*. Drain. Add ziti to sauce and mix well. Beat 6 eggs together; then combine with ziti mixture. Add 2 ounces Parmesan and blend well. Add ricotta at this point, if you choose. Place mixture in a lightly oiled 3-quart casserole. Preheat oven to 450°. Beat remaining 2 eggs together and pour over top. Sprinkle with remaining Parmesan. Bake for 30 minutes, until lightly browned. Allow to cool about 20 minutes before cutting. Yield: 6 to 8 servings.

"To reheat, place casserole in a larger pan of water and steam in a 250° oven until thoroughly warmed. Ziti refrigerates or freezes well and the flavor is definitely enhanced the second day."

Farla Zammit
THE B&B GROUP
(NEW YORKERS AT HOME) INC., NEW YORK

Miami Paella

A touch of Spain, Mexico, the Orient, India, and the great American West meld to form this international favorite with a special Miami flavor, enabling B&B hosts the opportunity to enjoy the world at their doorstep.

> 2 cans (7½ ounces each) chick peas, or 1½ cups chick peas, cooked
> 1 can (15 ounces) kidney beans, or 1½ cups kidney beans, cooked
> 1/4 teaspoon cumin
> 1 bay leaf
> 1/2 cup chopped onion
> 2 cloves garlic, minced
> 2 large green peppers, cut into strips
> 6 tomatoes, peeled and chopped
> Pinch of saffron
> Freshly ground pepper to taste
> 1/2 teaspoon oregano
> 1/2 teaspoon Tamari sauce
> 2 cups brown rice, cooked and drained
> 1 cup fresh peas, cooked
> Lemon wedges
> 1/2 cup pimiento

If using canned chick peas and kidney beans, drain, reserving all liquid. Otherwise, cook legumes according to package directions, reserving liquid. Place 1/4 cup reserved liquid in large skillet with cumin and bay leaf. Add onion, garlic and green pepper to skillet and simmer for 2 minutes, or until *al dente*.

Add chick peas, kidney beans, tomatoes, saffron, ground pepper, oregano and Tamari, simmering an additional 2 minutes. Remove bay leaf, and fold in rice and peas. Mix well, and turn into a 2-quart oven-proof casserole. Garnish with lemon wedges and pimiento. Heat in preheated 200° oven 15 minutes. Yield: 14 to 16 servings.

Olive Grethen, Host
BED & BREAKFAST CO., FLORIDA

Oysters Mosca

1/2 cup olive oil
1 large onion, chopped
4 garlic cloves, minced
1 pint fresh oysters, dry weight (or 2 pints canned, drained)
1/4 cup grated Parmesan cheese
1¼ cups Italian-style bread crumbs
4 strips bacon, cooked, drained and crumbled

Preheat oven to 325°. In medium saucepan saute onions and garlic in oil. Stir in oysters, cheese and bread crumbs. Place in a greased 1-quart casserole. Sprinkle with bacon. Bake for 30 minutes. Yield: 4 servings.

Shirley Jensen, Host
NEW ORLEANS BED & BREAKFAST, LOUISIANA

■ This dish is also a tempting hot hors d'oeuvre served with soda crackers. Its flavor is enhanced, according to one editor, by mixing one day, baking and serving the next.

Potato And Egg Bake

"Soaring mountains, roaring fires at the hearth add to the robust breakfasts of steaming cups of coffee and fresh country cream," and such hearty foods as this potato dish.

6 medium russet potatoes, washed
1/2 cup cracker crumbs
6 eggs, hard boiled and quartered
1¼ cup milk
1 cup sour cream
1/4 cup butter
Salt and pepper to taste

Preheat oven to 325°. Slice potatoes 1/4-inch thick. Sprinkle cracker crumbs on the bottom of a greased 8-inch square baking dish. Place half the potatoes and half the eggs in dish. Combine sour cream and 1/4 cup milk and pour half into dish. Repeat layers, ending with sour cream-milk mixture. Pour remaining cup milk over ingredients in baking dish. Sprinkle evenly with remaining crumbs, salt and pepper and dot with slivers of butter. Bake 45 minutes to 1 hour. Yield: 6 servings.

Darrell Trapp
"WHITNEYS' VILLAGE INN," NEW HAMPSHIRE

Prize Winning Sausage Squares

"May be served as an hors d'oeuvre. It also freezes well. Excellent with cold sliced oranges or melons in season. I serve scrambled eggs with this dish. Put parsley on side of plate. To make it special, sprinkle confectioners' sugar over the orange slices."

1 cup biscuit mix
1/3 cup milk
4 tablespoons mayonnaise
1 pound sausage
1/2 cup chopped onion
1 egg
2 cups sharp grated cheese
1 can (4 ounces) chopped chilies

Combine biscuit mix with milk and 2 tablespoons of mayonnaise and spread in 9- by 13-inch pan. Pat down. It will look lumpy. Cook the sausage with the chopped onion; drain and spread on top of biscuit dough. Mix together the egg, remaining mayonnaise, cheese and chilies and spread on top of sausage mixture. Bake in 350° oven for 25 minutes. Yield: 8 to 12 servings.

Mary Ann Peterson, Host
BED 'N BREAKFAST ASSOC., UTAH

Salmon Loaf

2 cups finely crushed corn flakes
1½ cups milk
2 cups cooked salmon, boned, flaked and chopped
1/3 cup sour cream
1 tablespoon chopped parsley
2 tablespoons chopped chives or minced onion
1 teaspoon salt
Dash of pepper
1/4 teaspoon thyme
1 tablespoon lemon juice
2 eggs, well beaten

Preheat oven to 375°. Combine corn flakes and milk in medium-size bowl; let stand for 10 minutes. Add salmon, sour cream, parsley, chives, salt, pepper, thyme and lemon juice and mix thoroughly. Fold in eggs. Turn mixture into well-greased 1-quart loaf pan. Bake for 1 hour. Yield: 6 to 8 servings.

*Serve with white sauce flavored with small amount of mustard.

Irene Pettigrew
STAY WITH A FRIEND, ALASKA

■ *See sauces following this recipe.

Sauces (White)

■ To make a medium white sauce, begin with . . .

1/4 cup butter
1/4 cup flour
1 teaspoon salt
Dash of white pepper
2 cups milk

Slowly melt butter in saucepan over low heat. Stir in flour and seasonings to make a smooth paste. Gradually add milk, stirring constantly. Cook over low heat until thickened. Yield: 2 cups.

For **cheese** sauce, add 1/2 teaspoon dry mustard and 2 cups grated cheese to prepared white sauce. Stir until cheese melts. (Serve over vegetables.)

Make a sauce for **fish** by adding 1/2 cup chopped parsley and 1/4 cup lemon juice to white sauce. Yield: 2½ cups.

Hot sauce for **beef** starts with the basic white sauce. Add to it 2 tablespoons horseradish, 2 teaspoons lemon juice and a dash of pepper sauce. Stir and heat through. Yield: 2 cups.

Make a **wine** sauce for **fish** by adding 2/3 cup dry white wine and 1 teaspoon basil to white sauce. Heat, pour over cooked fish and garnish with parsley.

The secret in making a really smooth sauce is in removing the pan from the heat before blending in the flour or milk. To reheat, use a double boiler.

Shrimp Sauce (For Fish)

2 tablespoons chopped green onions or shallots
1 tablespoon butter
1 tablespoon flour
1/4 teaspoon salt
1/2 cup heavy cream
3 tablespoons cream sherry
3 or 4 large gulf shrimp or 1/2 cup baby shrimp

Saute onions in butter 1 minute. Remove from heat and stir in flour and salt. Add cream and sherry gradually, stirring. Return to heat and simmer, stirring, until bubbly. Add shrimp and heat through. Pour over baked flounder or sole. Garnish with parsley, if desired. Yield: 2 to 4 servings.

Sandra Barker, Host
B&B PHILADELPHIA, PENNSYLVANIA

Salmon Supreme

3/4 cup butter
1/2 to 3/4 pounds fresh mushrooms, washed and sliced
6 small white onions, thinly sliced
1 jar (6 ounces) stuffed green olives, drained
2½ to 3 cups white wine
6 salmon slices, 3/4-inch thick
8 ounces sour cream

Melt butter in large skillet and saute mushrooms and onions. Stir in olives and white wine. Add salmon slices and cover. Simmer approximately 15 minutes, spooning sauce over fish, turning once. Remove salmon to serving platter; set aside and keep warm. Add sour cream to sauce, stir and heat over low heat. Spoon sauce over salmon. Yield: 6 servings.

"Serve over a bed of fluffy rice."

Chuck Barnett, Host
HOME SUITE HOMES, GEORGIA

■ "Extra sauce is delicious over green noodles, cooked broccoli and cauliflower."

Toad-In-A-Hole

"A breakfast or brunch favorite at our house, this traditional British dish is cooked sausage topped with Yorkshire pudding batter and baked. Also delicious as a light lunch or supper."

1 pound bulk sausage
4 eggs
1 cup milk
1 cup flour

Crumble and brown sausage in heavy iron skillet, or any heavy, high-sided frying pan, drain then place in 425° oven while you mix batter.

Put eggs in blender and blend on high for 1 minute. With blender still running, add milk slowly and then flour, 1 spoonful at a time. Blend for another 30 seconds. Remove pan from oven and pour batter over sausage. Return to oven and bake until golden brown and puffed up, about 20 to 25 minutes. Yield: 4 servings.

"Have everyone seated and ready to eat when you take this out of the oven and bring to table as it is at its height while piping hot. We serve with homemade maple, blueberry or raspberry syrup."

Sally B. Godfrey
BED & BREAKFAST DOWN EAST, LTD., MAINE

Vermont Chicken

1 egg, beaten
1¼ cups milk
3 pounds chicken, cut up
3/4 cup corn flake crumbs, seasoned to taste
5 tablespoons oil
1 cup light cream
1/2 cup maple syrup
Pineapple wedges
Currant jelly
Parsley sprigs

Preheat oven to 350°. Combine egg and 1/4 cup milk. Dip chicken pieces into egg mixture, then roll in crumbs. Heat oil in large skillet until just beginning to smoke. Place chicken in oil, reduce heat and fry until golden brown. Remove chicken to shallow baking dish. Combine remaining milk, cream and maple syrup; pour over chicken. Bake 30 minutes. Turn chicken over and bake an additional 30 minutes. Remove chicken to serving platter, garnish with pineapple wedges topped with a dollop of currant jelly and parsley sprigs. Yield: 4 servings.

"Delicious served with rice or sweet potatoes."
Louise Bouthillette, Host
"FOGGY HOLLOW DAIRY FARM IN FAIRFAX"
AMERICAN BED & BREAKFAST, VERMONT

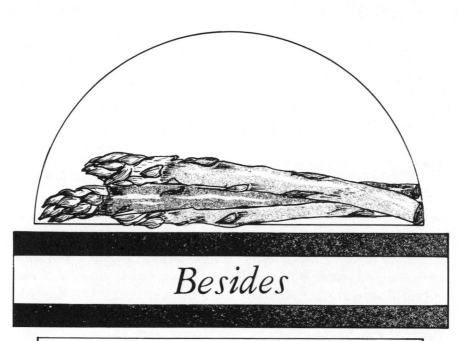

Besides

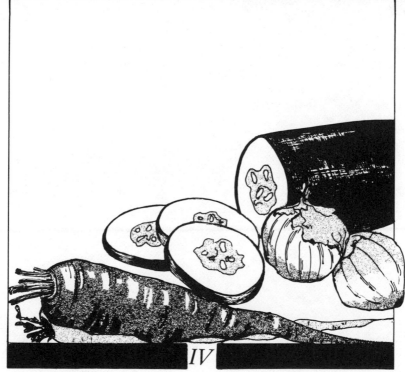

IV

Besides

WHILE *not fitting into any particular category, vegetables broaden the scope of any meal. At the breakfast table, these gifts from the harvest reflect pleasant living and a home-like ambience. These local side dishes are a welcome change to the habitual home fry.*

Traditional Southern recipes belong on any table, and provide a particularly nice addition to a holiday celebration. Assisting with the age-old dilemma of "what to serve with the main dish," these regional specialties introduce visiting guests to an extra benefit of the Bed and Breakfast experience by offering substantial accompaniment to any meal!

Baked Pineapple Souffle

3/4 cup sugar
1/4 pound butter, softened
4 eggs
1 can (16 ounces) crushed pineapple, drained
5 slices bread, cubed

Cream together sugar and butter in a medium-size mixing bowl. Add eggs and beat well. Add pineapple and beat in bread.

Pour into greased 1½-quart baking dish. Bake at 350° for 45 minutes or until browned. Yield: 6 to 8 servings.

■ This makes a wonderful accompaniment to the Easter ham.

Sue Carroll
THE MAINSTAY INN, NEW JERSEY

■ BED POST APPLESAUCE

Terry Kinsman, host of "The Felshaw Tavern" in Connecticut, suggests using apple cider instead of water and replacing the sugar with maple sugar.

It sounded like a good idea to us and this is what we came up with:

2 pounds apples
1/2 cup apple cider
1/2 cup maple syrup
1/2 teaspoon cinnamon (optional)
1/4 teaspoon nutmeg (optional)

Pare, core and cut apples into quarters. Bring cider to a boil in medium saucepan. Add apples and return to a boil. Reduce heat, cover and simmer 20 to 25 minutes, stirring occasionally. Add more cider if needed. Thoroughly blend in maple syrup. Season with cinnamon and nutmeg if desired. Yield: about 3 cups.

BED POST WRITERS GROUP

Cheese Pudding

5 slices bread, buttered
3/4 pound sharp Cheddar cheese, shredded
4 eggs, slightly beaten
2 cups milk
1/2 teaspoon dry mustard
1/2 teaspoon salt
Pinch cayenne pepper

Tear bread into small pieces and place in bottom of a greased 2-quart casserole. Sprinkle evenly with cheese. Combine eggs, milk, mustard, salt and cayenne. Pour over bread and cheese, pushing bread down so it is covered. Cover and refrigerate overnight.

Preheat oven to 350°. Place casserole in a pan of water and bake approximately 1 hour. Yield: 8 to 10 servings.

Anne Allison, Host
BED & BREAKFAST TEXAS STYLE

Corn Bread Dressing

5 cups crumbled corn bread
2 cups soft bread cubes
1/2 cup butter
1 ½ cups minced onion
1 ½ cups chopped celery
2 cups turkey stock
4 eggs, well beaten
1/2 cup milk
1 ½ teaspoons salt
1/4 teaspoon pepper

In large mixing bowl, combine corn bread and bread cubes. Melt butter in small saucepan; saute onion and celery until soft. Pour over bread mixture, alternately with turkey stock; stirring until well mixed. Combine eggs, milk and seasonings. Pour over mixture.

Add additional milk or turkey stock, if necessary, until mixture is the consistency of uncooked corn bread batter. Turn into a buttered 2-quart casserole. Bake in preheated 375° oven 40 minutes. Yield: 14 to 16 servings.

Mary Payne, Host
BED & BREAKFAST BIRMINGHAM, INC., ALABAMA

Crispy Corn Patties

1 egg
1 tablespoon flour
1/2 teaspoon sugar
1/4 teaspoon salt
1¼ cups creamed corn
Butter

Beat egg, flour, sugar and salt together. Blend in corn. Melt butter in skillet over medium heat. Drop batter by serving spoon into hot skillet. Saute patties until edges are crisp, turning once. Drain on paper toweling. Yield: 2 servings.

Kathleen Dexter
A REASONABLE ALTERNATIVE, INC.
BED & BREAKFAST ON LONG ISLAND, NEW YORK

Curried Fruit With Wine

"This is a wonderful accompaniment to ham, served in a crystal bowl on the buffet table. You can blend the drained fruit juices with other citrus juices for a fruit punch."

1 can (29 ounces) peach halves, drained
1 can (19 ounces) pear halves, drained
1 can (20 ounces) pineapple chunks, drained
2 cans (11 ounces each) mandarin oranges, drained
1 jar (8 ounces) maraschino cherries, drained
2 bananas, sliced
1/2 cup butter
1/2 cup brown sugar
1½ tablespoons curry powder
1½ cups dry white wine
1 tablespoon cornstarch

Place all fruit, except bananas, in shallow baking dish. Melt butter in saucepan and add sugar, curry and 1/2 cup wine. Cook, stirring, until sugar dissolves. Pour liquid over fruit and bake at 350° for 25 minutes.

Add bananas for the last 10 minutes of baking time. Strain liquid into a saucepan. Blend cornstarch with 3 tablespoons of wine and add to sauce, along with the rest of the wine. Cook until clear and pour over fruit. Serve hot or cold. Yield: About 10 cups.

Sandra Barker, Host
B&B OF PHILADELPHIA, PENNSYLVANIA

Frozen Cucumbers

4 medium cucumbers (about 8 cups), thinly sliced
1 medium onion, thinly sliced
1 tablespoon salt
1 cup white vinegar
2¼ cups sugar

Place cucumbers in large bowl with onion. Sprinkle salt over and mix well. Cover and refrigerate 2 hours or more. Drain off liquid. Combine vinegar and sugar. Pour over cucumbers and mix well. Place in freezer containers, proportionate in size to your needs, and freeze. Allow approximately 10 to 12 hours for freezing. Yield: 2 quarts.

Vanza Lazet, Host
BED & BREAKFAST OF PHILADELPHIA, PENNSYLVANIA

Gourmet Potatoes

"This is a convenient dish, as it can be made in advance and allowed to blend overnight. It's a great and different breakfast entree.

"Potatoes vary in size, and too many will make this casserole dry. So it's a matter of the cook's judgment as to how many to use."

6 medium potatoes, washed
2 cups shredded Cheddar cheese
1/4 cup butter, melted
1½ cups sour cream
1/2 cup minced onion
1/2 cup diced green pepper
1/2 cup chopped pimiento
1 teaspoon salt
1/4 teaspoon pepper
1/4 teaspoon paprika

Boil potatoes in their skins for 10 to 15 minutes. Cool, peel and shred. In large bowl, combine cheese, butter, sour cream, onion, green pepper, pimiento, salt, pepper and paprika. Stir in shredded potatoes until well combined. Spread mixture in a well-buttered 9- by 13- by 2-inch baking dish. Cover and refrigerate overnight.

When ready to use, bake, uncovered, in 350° oven for 30 minutes. Yield: 6 to 8 servings.

Sue, Host
BED & BREAKFAST ROCKY MOUNTAINS, COLORADO

Nookedly

1 package (12 ounces) wide noodles
1/2 pound bacon, diced
8 ounces cottage cheese
Salt and pepper to taste
Sour cream
Poppy seeds
Rye toast
Kosher pickles

Cook noodles according to package directions and drain. Fry bacon, add noodles to bacon and bacon fat. Mix in cottage cheese, salt and pepper. Serve hot, garnished with a dollop of sour cream and a sprinkling of poppy seeds. Serve on rye toast with Kosher pickles. Yield: 6 to 8 servings.

Nookedly may be prepared 24 hours in advance, refrigerated, and warmed in a 325° oven for approximately 1/2 hour.

Bobbi Seligman
SUNCOAST ACCOMMODATIONS, FLORIDA

Red Beans And Rice

■ Red Beans and Rice is a meal in itself, served with corn bread. Always put the hot sauce on the table, or serve with salsa, so guests can adjust the "bite" to their liking!

1 ham bone, or smoked ham hocks
2 teaspoons garlic salt
1/4 teaspoon Tabasco
1 teaspoon Worcestershire sauce
1 pound dried red beans
1 cup chopped celery
1 cup chopped onion
5 cloves garlic, minced
3 tablespoons vegetable oil
1 cup chopped ham, or hot or smoked sausage, chopped
2 bay leaves
Salt and coarsely ground pepper, to taste
4 cups white rice, cooked
1/4 cup minced parsley

Place ham bone, garlic salt, Tabasco, Worcestershire and beans in a large pot or Dutch oven. Cover with cold water and bring to simmer over low heat. Saute celery, onion and garlic in oil until onion is transparent.

Brown chopped ham or sausage, drain, and add to bean mixture, along with sauteed vegetables. Stir in bay leaves, salt and pepper. Continue to simmer until beans are soft and creamy,* approximately 2½ hours.

Meanwhile, prepare rice according to desired doneness. When beans are cooked, remove ham bone and bay leaves from pot. Stir in parsley, Spoon over hot fluffy rice. Yield: 8 to 10 servings.

Shirley Jensen, Host
NEW ORLEANS BED & BREAKFAST, LOUISIANA

■ *Leave cover off the pot the last hour as the old-timers do.

Sue's Spoon Bread

2 cups boiling water
1 cup cornmeal
1 teaspoon salt
1/2 cup butter
2 eggs, beaten
2 cups milk, scalded
1 teaspoon butter

Preheat oven to 400°. In medium bowl, pour water over cornmeal and salt, mixing well. Stir in butter until melted. Add eggs and milk, combining thoroughly. Pour into a buttered 1½-quart oven-proof casserole. Bake 40 minutes. Yield: 10 to 12 servings.

Lyn Benson
"BENSONHOUSE OF RICHMOND," VIRGINIA

■ We like this spoonbread served warm with melted butter and hot maple syrup poured over the top. In Charleston, S.C., a cup of grits (cooked according to package directions) is added to their spoonbread.

Sweet Potato Casserole

2 pounds sweet potatoes (3 or 4 large)*
1½ cups sugar
2 eggs, beaten
1/2 cup milk
1/2 cup softened butter
1/4 teaspoon nutmeg
1/2 teaspoon cinnamon

For topping:
1/4 cup butter, melted
1/2 cup chopped pecans
1/2 cup brown sugar
1/2 cup crushed cornflakes

Boil potatoes in water to cover for 30 minutes. Drain, cool, peel and slice into 1/2-inch circles. Mix together with sugar, eggs, milk, butter, nutmeg and cinnamon. Spread in a greased 1½-quart baking dish. Bake in a 350° oven for 30 minutes.

Mix together melted butter, nuts, brown sugar and cereal, spread over potatoes and bake for 15 minutes longer. Yield: 6 to 8 servings.

*Canned sweet potatoes may be substituted. Spread topping on at beginning of cooking time and bake for a total of 30 minutes.

Shirley Jensen, Host
NEW ORLEANS BED & BREAKFAST, LOUISIANA

Tomato Pudding

"A favorite served for dinner, as well as brunch, in our Bed & Breakfast household!"

> 1 can (10 ounces) tomato puree
> 1 cup brown sugar
> 1/2 teaspoon salt
> 1/2 cup boiling water
> 1/3 cup melted butter
> 2 cups fresh bread cubes

Preheat oven to 350°. Combine tomato puree, sugar, salt and water in medium saucepan. Simmer 5 minutes. Stir in melted butter. Spread bread cubes on bottom of a greased 1½-quart oven-proof casserole. Top with tomato mixture. Cover and bake 30 minutes. (If extra crispness is desired, bake uncovered.) Yield: 4 to 6 servings.

Linda Fellour
THE BED & BREAKFAST LEAGUE, LTD.
WASHINGTON, D.C.

■ Grandmother always served this dish with broiled fish. Sometimes she used raisin bread cubes. 'Tis sweet, but so good!

Wind Ridge Chutney

"Traditionally this is made in mid-October, when the Northern Spy apples (firm, tart, solid—a lovely all-purpose apple) are ready. By this time our tomato vines, laden with ripening fruit, are pulled and hung from the beams in our cold cellar and the garden is being put to bed for the winter. The woodstove has been lighted to take the chill off our cedar log home and is burning just right to simmer this family favorite for four days. When the Chutney is ready to bottle and seal, the whole house is permeated with the piquant aroma—delightful!"

A four-day project:
First day: Mix in a large kettle, using long-handled wooden spoon:

> 5 to 6 quarts ripe tomatoes, diced
> 4 oranges, sliced, seeded and cut into small pieces
> 6 lemons, sliced, seeded and cut into small pieces
> 2 limes, sliced, seeded and cut into small pieces
> 10 medium onions, peeled and sliced
> 4 large green peppers, seeded and chopped
> 1 whole head of garlic cloves, peeled and minced
> 3 pounds raisins
> 1 pound currants
> 6 tablespoons candied ginger, diced

Scald and add to the above mixture:

- 3 cups cider vinegar
- 2 pounds brown sugar
- 3 cups white sugar
- 1 tablespoon cinnamon
- 1 teaspoon *each,* ground cloves, ginger, allspice, nutmeg
- 2 teaspoons cayenne pepper
- 2 tablespoons dry English mustard (Colman's)
- 3 tablespoons curry powder
- 20-24 apples*

Bring the whole mixture to a boil and boil gently for about an hour, stirring every few minutes. Cover the kettle, push to back (cool) corner of stove. If using a wood stove, it is assumed at this time of year you will let stove go out at night. Let stand overnight to cool.

Second day: Bring to boil, simmer for about 3/4 hour, stirring often. Cover, cool, let stand overnight.

Third day: Repeat simmering, stirring. Cover, cool, let stand overnight.

*Fourth day: Core, slice and cut up into small pieces about 20 medium-sized tart, firm apples (Northern Spy or Cortlands). Add to mixture (which by now will smell heavenly). Heat to boil and cook gently until apples are transparent and soft (but not mushy) and until liquid from kettle will crinkle when a few drops are poured on a cold saucer, about 3/4 to 1 hour.

Stir well every few minutes during this last simmering. Put in 10-12 sterile pint jars and seal. ("The number of jars depends on amounts of apples, oranges, etc., you may have on hand and use. Each time I make it my amounts are different.") Let "age" for a couple of weeks and flavors mingle before using (if you can).

"We have used this in many ways. It is very tasty on whole wheat bread with creamed cheese for sandwiches, excellent warmed and spooned over homemade vanilla ice cream, or swirled through vanilla pudding before chilling, and, of course, is a must with curried dishes."

Sally B. Godfrey
BED & BREAKFAST DOWN EAST, LTD., MAINE

Beyonds (Desserts)

V

Beyonds

BREAKFAST like a king, lunch like a prince, and dinner like a pauper, the saying goes. To make it a "regal" breakfast, B&B hosts go beyond the basics. The finishing delights to their great homemade meals are found in this chapter of cakes, pies and sweets.

To some, desserts are simple treats; to others, these delicacies are the most important aspect of the meal. It's these diners who feel that Beverages, Brunch Main Dishes, and Besides orbit around the BEYONDS.

The confections presented here are testimony to America's European heritage with Linzer and Bienenstich. Tennessee Walking Pound Cake, Berkshire Bed and Breakfast Bundt and Amish Vanilla Pie portray regional "Land of the Free" bounty. Made ahead and awaiting a festive occasion is Moose Mincemeat.

One of the most important roles of Beyonds is to satisfy the midnight snacker; however, these are an equally important addition to morning juice and coffee, and an elegant finish to a sit-down meal!

Amish Vanilla Pie

Filling:
1/2 cup sugar
2 tablespoons flour
1 egg
1/2 cup dark corn syrup
1 cup water
1 teaspoon vanilla

Crumb Topping:
1 cup flour
1/2 cup brown sugar
1/2 teaspoon cream of tartar
1/2 teaspoon baking soda
1/2 cup butter

1 9-inch pie shell

Combine filling ingredients in saucepan, and bring to full boil over medium heat, stirring constantly. Remove from heat; set aside to cool. (Filling will become thick.) Mix ingredients for crumb topping together, using hands or food processor, until combined to crumb stage.

Pour cooled filling into pie shell. Sprinkle with crumb topping. Bake at 350° for 40 minutes. Yield: 6 to 8 servings.

Mary Darlington, Host
BED & BREAKFAST OF PHILADELPHIA, PENNSYLVANIA

■ Sprinkle allspice on bottom of pie shell for a nutty flavor.

Berkshire Bed And Breakfast Bundt

"We prepare this the night before and serve it to our guests on a warming tray for breakfast. They always ask for the recipe."

1/2 cup margarine
1 cup sugar
2 eggs
1 teaspoon almond extract
2 cups flour
1 teaspoon baking powder
1 teaspoon baking soda
1/2 teaspoon salt
8 ounces sour cream
1 can (16 ounces) whole cranberry sauce
1/2 cup chopped nuts

Preheat oven to 350°. Grease a Bundt pan. Cream margarine and sugar together in large mixing bowl. Beat in eggs and extract. Sift flour, baking powder, soda and salt together. Mix alternately into batter with sour cream. Pour 1/2 the mixture into prepared pan. Combine cranberry sauce and nuts in small bowl, spreading 1/2 over batter in pan to within 1/4 inch of outer edge. Top with remaining batter, then with remaining cranberry sauce. Bake 35 to 40 minutes, or until done in center. Yield: 14 to 16 servings.

Tim and Mary Allen
BERKSHIRE BED & BREAKFAST CONNECTION, MASSACHUSETTS

Bienenstich

■ Bruni has translated her family recipes from German into English. Be sure to look up Linzer Torte in this chapter.

3½ ounces cottage cheese, well pressed out
4 tablespoons milk
4 tablespoons vegetable oil
2 well-heaped tablespoons sugar
Pinch of salt
7 ounces plain flour (3/4 cup)
4 level teaspoons Oetker Baking Powder Backin*

For Topping:
1¾ to 2½ ounces butter (2 to 4 tablespoons)
3½ ounces sugar (1/3 cup)
1 packet Oetker Vanillin Sugar*
1 tablespoon milk
3½ ounces almonds, blanched and thinly sliced

To prepare pastry, rub the cottage cheese, if desired, through a fine sieve and mix with the milk, oil, sugar and salt. Sieve the flour and Bakin together. Add to the mixed ingredients, a little at a time, until slightly more than half has been used. Knead in the rest of the flour. Grease a 10-inch round cake tin with a removable rim (spring-form pan), and roll out pastry to fit the base.

To prepare the topping, melt together butter, sugar and vanillin sugar, and add the milk. Stir in the almonds and set aside to cool. If it should be too firm when cold, add a little milk. Spread evenly over the pastry. Bake in a moderately hot (375°) oven for about 20 minutes. Cool, and fill with buttercream, if desired. Recipe for buttercream follows.

■ *Available in gourmet food shops.

Buttercream Filling

1/2 packet Oetker Pudding Powder,* vanilla flavor
2 well-heaped tablespoons sugar
1/2 pint cold milk (1 cup)
3½ ounces butter (7 tablespoons)

Combine buttercream ingredients in a small saucepan and stir over low heat until thickened. When cake is quite cold, cut it horizontally into halves, spread the filling on the bottom half, and lay the other on top.

Bruni Fehner
A&A BED & BREAKFAST OF FLORIDA

■ *Available in gourmet food shops.

Bourbon Pie

■ Bourbon pie is a Southern tradition served at "Anchuca" – which is Indian for "Happy Home." Guests are treated to a Southern-style breakfast, a tour of this restored 1830's mansion, use of pool and hot tub and lots of Southern hospitality.

1/2 package (8½ ounces) chocolate wafers
3 tablespoons melted butter
1 can (14 ounces) sweetened condensed milk (not evaporated)
21 marshmallows
1/2 pint whipping cream
3 tablespoons bourbon

Heavy whipping cream, whipped (optional)
Maraschino cherries (optional)

Crush wafers into crumbs and mix with butter. Saving 1/2 cup of crumbs for topping, spread the rest in an 8-inch pie pan and bake in 350° oven for 5 minutes. Cool.

To prepare filling, mix milk and marshmallows in top of a double boiler. Heat over hot (not boiling) water until smooth, stirring occasionally. Cool. Whip cream and add bourbon. Fold into cooled marshmallow mixture and pour into pie shell. Sprinkle the reserved crumbs on top. Chill thoroughly. Serve with whipped cream and a cherry on top, if desired. "Placing a mint leaf on the side is a nice touch." Yield: 6 servings.

"ANCHUCA," MISSISSIPPI

Bread Pudding With Whiskey Sauce

1 loaf French bread
1 quart milk
3 eggs
2 cups sugar
2 tablespoons vanilla
1 cup raisins
1 tablespoon nutmeg
3 tablespoons butter

Whiskey Sauce:
1/2 cup butter
1 cup sugar
1 egg, well beaten
1/2 cup bourbon, or to taste

Preheat oven to 350°. Tear bread into a medium-size bowl. Pour milk over and mix well; set aside to soak 5 to 10 minutes. Combine eggs, sugar, vanilla, raisins and nutmeg. Add to bread mixture, stirring until well combined. Melt butter in a 1½-quart baking dish. Pour in bread mixture. Bake 45 minutes, or until firm.

Meanwhile, to prepare whiskey sauce, dissolve butter and sugar in top of double boiler. When very hot, add egg and whisk fast so sauce doesn't curdle. Cool, and stir in bourbon. Remove pudding from oven and allow to cool. Divide into desired portions and serve with warm sauce. Yield: 6 to 8 servings.

Shirley Jensen, Host
New Orleans Bed & Breakfast, Louisiana

■ Whiskey sauce is also tasty over rice pudding, angel food or pound cake, devil's food cake and brownies

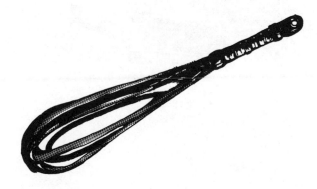

Chocolate Silk Pie

1 package (16 ounces) cream-filled chocolate cookies
1/4 cup butter, softened

Filling:
1 cup sugar
2 packets (1 ounce each) liquid chocolate flavor
1 ounce unsweetened chocolate, melted
6 ounces butter, softened
3 eggs

Process cookies to crumbs in blender. Add butter. Press into 9-inch pie pan to form a crust. Refrigerate until ready to fill.

To prepare filling, cream together sugar, both chocolates and butter until smooth. Add eggs and whip at high speed, approximately 4 to 8 minutes, until mixture peaks. Spread into prepared pie crust and freeze. Yield: 8 to 10 servings.

Ted and Sharon Wroblewski
"THE BERNERHOF INN," NEW HAMPSHIRE

■ Serve with dollop of whipped cream and shaved chocolate or crushed nuts on top.

Cold Raspberry Souffle

This is a versatile souffle that's popular with hosts. It can be featured for breakfast, or served frozen at snack time with small crisp cookies, as well as being a delightful dessert. It's a special treat that brings a festive air to the breakfast table.

2 packages unflavored gelatin
Pinch of salt
3 tablespoons cold water
2 pints fresh* raspberries, washed and drained
1 tablespoon lemon juice
1/2 cup sugar
2 tablespoons Kirsch liqueur (optional)
3 egg whites
1 cup heavy cream, whipped
1/4 cup toasted, slivered almonds

In small saucepan, soften gelatin in cold, salted water over low heat; stir to dissolve. Reserve 8 whole berries for garnish. Puree remaining berries in blender or food processor. Press puree through a sieve to remove seeds. Combine dissolved gelatin with puree, lemon juice and sugar in a bowl and place over ice until thickened, stirring often. Blend in kirsch, if desired. Beat egg whites until stiff, and fold into berry mixture, along with whipped cream. Spoon into individual dessert dishes, and chill for 2 hours or longer. To serve, place a raspberry in center of each and sprinkle with almonds. Yield: 8 servings.

Darrell Trapp
"WHITNEYS' VILLAGE INN," NEW HAMPSHIRE

■ *If using frozen berries, you will need one 10-ounce package. Drain before using and omit the sugar called for in recipe.
This souffle can also be made in an oiled 2-quart souffle mold. Chill for at least 3 hours. Unmold and garnish with extra whipped cream, whole berries and almonds. Serve with several choices of coffee cakes.

Countryside Fresh Apple Cake

"Countryside is a Bed and Breakfast guesthome located on a quiet, tree-lined side street in the charming rural village of Summit Point, West Virginia. near historic Harpers Ferry. Since the village is surrounded by apple orchards, this Fresh Apple Cake recipe is especially appropriate."

4 cups unpeeled apples, chopped and cored
3 eggs, beaten
1 cup oil
2 cups flour
2 cups sugar
1 teaspoon salt
1½ teaspoons baking soda
1 teaspoon cinnamon
Cinnamon and sugar mixture (enough to coat pan)

Combine apples, eggs and oil in a mixing bowl. In another bowl combine flour, sugar, salt, baking soda and cinnamon. Stir flour mixture into apples, mixing well.

Oil a sheet, tube pan or two 9-inch bread pans thoroughly. Coat pan completely with the sugar/cinnamon mixture. Turn batter into pan and bake at 350° for 60 minutes. Yield: 8 servings.

Lisa Hileman
"COUNTRYSIDE," WEST VIRGINIA

Cranberry Short Cake

2 cups cranberries, washed and drained
1 cup sugar, or more to taste
1/2 teaspoon cinnamon
1/2 cup chopped walnuts
2 eggs, beaten
1 cup flour
3/4 cup butter, melted

Preheat oven to 325°. Grease a 10-inch pie pan and place cranberries on bottom. Combine 1/3 cup sugar with cinnamon and walnuts. Sprinkle over cranberries. Beat remaining 2/3 cup of sugar into the eggs, along with flour and butter. Pour batter over cranberries. Bake approximately 1 hour, or until crust is nicely browned. Yield: 6 to 8 servings.

Karen Koziara, Host
BED & BREAKFAST OF PHILADELPHIA, PENNSYLVANIA

■ Serve warm at tea time or a la mode for dessert. Great with a game bird dinner.

Crunchy Apple Pie

"In the days before refrigeration and freezers, people found, by trial and error, ways to safely keep food.

"The old-order Amish here pick their apples, peel and quarter them, string them on a cord and hang them in the kitchen to dry. Once dry, 'schnitz' become winter pies."

>30 pieces schnitz (dried apples), soaked overnight, or 6 apples, cored, peeled
>	and sliced
>1 10-inch pie shell
>1 cup graham cracker crumbs
>1 cup sugar
>1/2 cup flour
>1/2 cup walnuts. chopped
>1/2 teaspoon cinnamon
>1/4 teaspoon salt
>1/2 cup melted butter

Arrange apples in pie shell. Combine cracker crumbs, sugar, flour, nuts, cinnamon and salt in bowl. Sprinkle over apples. Pour melted butter evenly over top of pie. Bake at 350°, 1 hour. Yield: 6 to 8 servings.

"Top with ice cream or whipped cream."

Burretta Redhead
"MASON HOUSE INN," IOWA

Linzer Torte

■ Here's another of Bruni Fehner's family recipes, translated from German. (Also see page 143.)

> 7 ounces plain flour (3/4 cup)
> 1 level teaspoon Oetker Baking Powder Backin*
> 4½ ounces sugar (2/3 cup)
> 1 packet Oetker Vanillin Sugar*
> 2 drops Oetker Baking Essence, bitter almond flavor* (or 1/4 teaspoon almond extract)
> Pinch ground cloves
> 1 level teaspoon ground cinnamon
> 1 egg white
> 1/2 egg yolk
> 4½ ounces butter (1 stick + 1 tablespoon)
> 4½ ounces ground almonds or hazelnuts (1/2 cup)
> About 3½ ounces jam
> 1/2 egg yolk + 1 teaspoon milk

For the pastry, mix and sieve (sift) together the flour and the backin onto a pastry board or cool slab. Make a well in the center and pour in sugar, vanillin sugar, spices, egg white and 1/2 egg yolk. Draw in some of the flour from the sides of the well and mix with these to form a thickish paste.

Add the cold fat (butter), cut into small pieces, and the ground almonds or hazelnuts. Cover the whole with more of the flour. Starting from the middle, work all these ingredients quickly, with the hands, into a smooth firm paste. If it should be sticky, cool thoroughly for some time. [The author refrigerated this dough 4 hours, and found it becomes softer and more pliable the more it is handled.]

Roll out a little less than half the pastry to the same size as the base of a round cake tin with a removable rim, diameter of 10½ inches (spring form pan), and then cut it into 16 to 20 equal narrow strips. Roll out the rest of the pastry to line the base of the round cake tin. Spread with the jam, leaving 1/2 inch free around the edge. Make a criss-cross pattern over the jam with the strips of pastry and brush these with egg yolk and milk beaten together. Bake in moderately hot (375°) oven for 25 minutes. Yield: 6 to 8 servings.

Bruni Fehner
A&A BED & BREAKFAST OF FLORIDA

■ *May be found in specialty food shops or gourmet shops.

Minute Mousse

1 package (6 ounces) chocolate chips
3/4 cup + 1 tablespoon milk
1/2 teaspoon instant coffee
2 eggs
3 tablespoons rum or brandy
Whipped cream and sifted cocoa (optional)

Place chocolate chips in blender. Scald milk; stir in coffee. Add milk to chocolate; blend until smooth. With blender motor running, add eggs and rum or brandy. Pour into demitasse cups and chill. To serve, top with whipped cream and a light sifting of cocoa. Yield: 5 servings.

Lillian Marshall
KENTUCKY HOMES B&B, KENTUCKY

■ Lil serves this to guests at Derby time. It is an elegant finale to any breakfast party, and so simple to prepare.

Moose Meat Mincemeat

■ Mincemeat began as a way of preserving meats— venison, bear, moose buffalo, veal or lamb, etc.— by our ancestors. It was actually pickling of meats with various herbs, spices and vinegars. As our society "matured," more vegetables and fruits were added.The "meat" aspect for entree "pyes" of old England decreased until, as we know it today, "mincemeat" is for dessert pies, and such . . . now associated with holidays and gift giving.

> 1 pound moose meat*
> 1/2 pound beef suet
> 4 apples, peeled, cored and finely chopped
> 1 quince, finely chopped
> 1¾ cups sugar
> 1/2 cup molasses
> 1 pint cider
> 1 pound raisins
> 3/4 pound currants†
> 1 tablespoon finely chopped citron
> 1/2 pint cooking brandy (1 cup)
> 1 teaspoon cinnamon
> 1 teaspoon mace
> 1 teaspoon cloves
> 1 teaspoon nutmeg
> 1/4 teaspoon pepper
> Salt to taste

Cover meat and suet with boiling water, and simmer until tender (about 2 hours). Leave in cooking liquid to cool. When cool, remove layer of fat (skim). Reserving stock, remove meat and suet and chop fine. Place in large pot, add apple, quince, sugar, molasses, cider, raisins, currants and citron. Reduce reserved stock in which meat and suet were cooked to 1½ cups. Add to the fruit and meat mixture. Heat slowly, stirring occasionally, and simmer 2 hours in slow cooker. Add brandy and spices.

Seal in sterilized pint jars, while boiling hot. Store and use for pies as needed. Yield: 7 to 8 pints.

*Or venison or beef.

†Substitute equal amount of golden raisins if currants are unavailable.

Irene Pettigrew
"STAY WITH A FRIEND," ALASKA

■ Breakfast Turnovers can easily be made by placing 2 tablespoons mincemeat in middle of a pie-dough square. Fold in half to make a triangle, and crimp edges with a fork. Brush pastry with melted butter and bake at 400° for 10 minutes.

Heat 1/2 cup chopped nuts with 1 pint mincemeat. Stir in 1/2 cup sherry and serve hot over ice cream.

Oatmeal Coconut Cookies

"I had a young divorced father and his two small sons, aged 2½ and 5½, from Quebec, Canada. The first evening I offered them my homemade cookies. They could reply only in French. The father then said their answer was 'no,' because they would have to brush their teeth again.

"The following morning at the breakfast table they, again, spoke to me in French, and with their father's translation they replied, 'We'll take our cookies now!'"

These cookies also make a nice snack to pack and send along with departing guests.

> 3/4 cup sifted flour
> 1/2 teaspoon salt
> 1/2 teaspoon baking soda
> 1/2 cup soft butter or margarine
> 1/2 cup sugar
> 1/2 cup brown sugar, tightly packed
> 1 egg, well beaten
> 1 teaspoon vanilla
> 1/2 cup rolled oats
> 1/2 cup coconut
> 1/2 cup chopped nuts

Preheat oven to 350°. Sift together flour, salt and baking soda; set aside. Cream butter and sugars together in large bowl. Add egg and mix well. Stir in vanilla and sifted ingredients, mixing well. Fold in oats, coconut and nuts.* Drop by teaspoonfuls, 2 inches apart, onto greased cookie sheets. Bake on middle rack 10 to 12 minutes. Yield: 3 dozen.

Esther O'Neil, Host
RENT-A-ROOM INTERNATIONAL
BED & BREAKFAST IN SOUTHERN CALIFORNIA

■ *Adding 1/2 cup raisins or chocolate chips is appealing to cookie lovers.

Peanut Butter Buckeyes

2 cups butter
2 pounds peanut butter
3 pounds confectioners' sugar
1 package (12 ounces) semi-sweet chocolate bits
1/3 stick of parafin

Cream butter; then cream in peanut butter. Add sugar and continue to beat. (Mixture will be stiff.)

Roll mixture into small, walnut-size balls. Place on wax paper on cookie sheet or tray. Chill for several hours or overnight.

Melt the chocolate bits and parafin in the top of a double boiler. Dip chilled balls into chocolate with a toothpick, leaving top open for the "eye" of the buckeye. (When you remove the toothpick, smooth over the hole.) Yield: About 14 dozen buckeyes!

Recipe may be cut in half.

Sally Hollenback
BUCKEYE BED & BREAKFAST, OHIO

■ Replace the traditional mints with these surprise candies on guests' pillows for "Sweet Dreams"!

Pecan Tarts

Crust:
1/2 cup butter, at room temperature
3 ounces cream cheese, soften to room temperature
1 cup sifted flour

Filling:
1 cup coarsely chopped pecans
1 large egg, slightly beaten
3/4 cup packed brown sugar
1 tablespoon melted butter
Dash salt
Few drops vanilla

Cream together softened butter and cream cheese. Add flour, 1/2 at a time, mixing well. Chill dough. When ready to use roll out dough, 1/2 at a time, on a floured surface. Cut out circles a little larger than tart pans, and mold them into the tart pans.

Sprinkle a few nuts in bottom of tart pans. Mix together egg, sugar, melted butter, salt and vanilla. Pour 1 tablespoon of filling mixture over nuts, and sprinkle more nuts on top.

Arrange tart pans on cookie sheet and bake in a 350° oven for 15 to 17 minutes. Reduce oven heat to 250° and continue to bake for 10 to 20 minutes, or until done. They are done when they lift easily out of the pans. Remove to a cooling rack. Yield: 2 dozen.

Sally Hollenback
BUCKEYE BED & BREAKFAST, OHIO

Pumpkin Cake With Cream Cheese Frosting

2 cups sugar
4 eggs
1 cup vegetable oil
1 can (16 ounces) pumpkin
2 cups flour
2½ teaspoons cinnamon
1/4 teaspoon nutmeg
1/4 teaspoon allspice
2 teaspoons baking soda
1/2 teaspoon salt

Frosting:
1/2 cup margarine, softened
1 cup confectioners' sugar
8 ounces cream cheese, softened
2 teaspoons vanilla

1 cup chopped nuts

Preheat oven to 350°. Grease and lightly flour a 9- by 13- by 2-inch pan. Combine 2 cups sugar, eggs, oil, pumpkin, flour, cinnamon, nutmeg, allspice, baking soda and salt in large bowl, and mix well. Pour batter into prepared pan. Bake 35 minutes, or until a fork inserted comes out clean.

Meanwhile, prepare frosting by combining margarine, confectioners' sugar, cream cheese and vanilla in a large mixing bowl. Beat until smooth.

Place cake on rack to cool. Spread cooled cake with frosting and sprinkle top with nuts. Yield: 6 servings.

"This cake freezes well when unfrosted."

Paul and Judy Barker
LOCH LYME LODGE AND COTTAGES, NEW HAMPSHIRE

S. C. H. Brownies

4 squares bitter-sweet chocolate
1/2 cup butter
2 cups sugar
1 cup flour
Pinch of salt
6 ounces chopped pecans or walnuts
4 eggs
1 tablespoon vanilla
1 tablespoon cinnamon

Preheat oven to 250°. Melt chocolate and butter together in top of double boiler, stirring to combine. Mix sugar, flour, salt, nuts, eggs and vanilla together lightly. Blend into chocolate mixture. Pour batter into well-buttered 10- by 14- by 2-inch baking dish. Bake 1 hour for a "gooey" consistency. A little longer for a cake-like brownie. Yield: 3 dozen 2-inch squares.

"We sometimes put a peppermint topper on these." After removing brownies from oven, evenly place 10 chocolate-covered mint candy patties on top. Return to oven for 2 to 3 minutes, allowing chocolate to melt. Remove, and spread topping with metal spatula or knife, heating spatula under hot water to ease spreading.*

Barbara Hershey
"STODDARD-COOPER HOUSE"
AN INTIMATE INN, GEORGIA

■ Sprinkle warm brownies with confectioners' sugar, cut into squares and remove from pan while still warm.

*Allow frosted brownies to cool slightly, then cut into squares quickly, before frosting hardens.

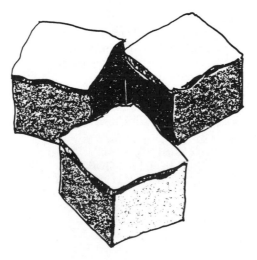

Shortcrust Pie Crust

2 cups flour
1/4 teaspoon salt
Pinch of baking powder
1 egg yolk
1 tablespoon lemon juice
1 cup water, cold
1/2 cup cold butter

Sift together flour, salt and baking powder into a chilled bowl. In another small chilled bowl, lightly beat ice water, egg yolk and lemon juice to mix well. Add butter, in small amounts, to flour, cutting in with a pastry blender or two knives. When butter-flour mixture has been reduced to small beads, add liquid in drips and mix with pastry blender. You may not need entire amount of liquid.

When dough is neither too crumbly nor too sticky, form into a ball. Dough may be stored in refrigerator at this stage, or roll out for use. Yield: one 10-inch pie crust.

Sandra Barker, Host
BED & BREAKFAST PHILADELPHIA, PENNSYLVANIA

Water Whip Pie Crust

3/4 cup shortening
1/4 cup water, boiling
1 tablespoon milk
2 cups flour
1 teaspoon salt
Sugar (optional)

Beat shortening, water and milk with a fork until whipped cream stage. Mix in flour and salt. Roll out dough between sheets of wax paper. Yields top and bottom for one 9-inch pie crust. Brush top crust with milk and sprinkle with sugar (optional).

Sandra Barker, Host
BED & BREAKFAST PHILADELPHIA, PENNSYLVANIA

Tennessee Walking Pound Cake

1 cup butter
2 cups sugar
1/2 cup brown sugar
6 eggs
3 cups cake flour, sifted
2 teaspoons baking powder
1 teaspoon salt
1 teaspoon freshly grated nutmeg
1 cup sour cream
1/2 cup bourbon whiskey
1 cup finely chopped pecans
Confectioners' sugar
1 teaspoon grated orange rind

Preheat oven to 325°. Thoroughly cream together butter and sugars until light and fluffy. Add eggs, one at a time, beating continuously. Sift together flour, baking powder, salt and nutmeg. Blend sour cream and bourbon together. Add alternately with dry ingredients to batter, stirring well after each addition. Fold in pecans. Pour batter into a buttered Bundt pan. Bake 1 hour and 25 minutes. Turn onto wire rack to cool. Combine orange rind and confectioners' sugar. Sprinkle over cake. Yield: 14 to 16 servings.

Betty Cordellos
NASHVILLE BED & BREAKFAST, TENNESSEE

■ Frost cake with a glaze made with enough bourbon whiskey and confectioners' sugar to reach a glaze consistency. Decorate cake top with pecan halves.

Bits and Bites

VI

Bits and Bites

BREAKFAST appetizers at the ready for late arriving or unexpected guests are popular with B&B hosts. A healthier, slimmer and trimmer attitude is in vogue and, with artful treatment, these miscellaneous recipes become earthy but light party fare for many occasions. (One host syggests fresh tomato wedges, green pepper strips, chinese cabbage chunks, diet crisp crackers and pear slices to dip into a bowl of yogurt spiked with sweet relish and a dash of horseradish.)

Nibbling pleases the guest until the last minute kitchen duties are completed, and a platter of these canapes adds an extra touch to an extended meal or brunch.

Carolyn's Elegant Puffs

1 loaf (16 ounces) unsliced bread
6 ounces cream cheese, softened
1 cup butter
1/2 pound sharp Cheddar cheese, grated
4 egg whites, stiffly beaten

Remove crust from bread. Cut loaf into 1-inch cubes; set aside. In top of double boiler, over boiling water, melt together cream cheese, butter and Cheddar, whipping to combine. Remove from heat and fold in egg whites. With a fork, carefully dip cubes into "fondue," coating each cube completely. Place cubes 1/2 inch apart on greased cookie sheet and freeze. When frozen, transfer cubes to plastic freezer bags.

To serve, preheat oven to 400°. Place desired amount of frozen cubes onto greased cookie sheet and bake 10 to 12 minutes or until lightly browned. Yield: 70 "puffs."

CAROLYN'S BED & BREAKFAST HOMES
IN SAN DIEGO, CALIFORNIA

■ These puffs are delightful for nibblers, or as "croutons" for spinach salads. Variations on this theme . . . Add 1 cup finely grated pecans or 1/2 package dry onion soup mix to cheese mixture just before dipping process. Sprinkle the onion-flavored puffs with paprika before freezing.

Caviar Pie

5 or 6 hard-cooked eggs, peeled and chopped
2 teaspoons minced onion
2 tablespoons mayonnaise
1 jar (4 ounces) caviar
3 ounces cream cheese
3/4 cup sour cream
Minced watercress
Rye or pumpernickel party bread slices

Combine eggs and onion in medium bowl. Stir in mayonnaise slowly to make a firm egg salad. Press mixture onto bottom of 6-inch pie plate or ramekin. Spread caviar over egg salad to within 1/2 inch of edge; set aside in refrigerator. In small mixing bowl, beat cream cheese and sour cream together until smooth. Delicately frost the pie with the cheese mixture, concealing caviar. Make a decorative border with watercress around pie rim. Cover loosely and refrigerate up to several hours. *Will not* keep overnight! Serve with rye or pumpernickel party bread. Yield: 8 to 10 servings.

Wendy Berry, Host
THE B&B GROUP (NEW YORKERS
AT HOME) INC., NEW YORK

Chili Nuts

1 tablespoon peanut oil
1 egg white
2 teaspoons chili powder
1 teaspoon ground cumin
1 teaspoon garlic salt
1 tablespoon onion powder
1/8 teaspoon hot pepper sauce
1 pound unsalted dry-roasted peanuts

Preheat oven to 325°. Grease bottom of a 15½- by 10½-inch jelly roll pan or baking sheet with peanut oil. In medium bowl, beat egg white until foamy. Fold in chili powder, cumin, garlic salt, onion powder and hot pepper sauce. Add peanuts; stir to coat evenly. Spread peanuts on pan in single layer. Bake for 20 minutes. Remove from oven and separate if necessary. Store in airtight container. Yield: 1 pound.

Paula Gris, Madalyne Eplan and Jane Carney
BED & BREAKFAST ATLANTA, GEORGIA

■ Great topper for steamed green beans or broccoli, and Colonial Peanut Soup (See page 20).

Faye's Caramel Corn

Serve in small dishes on the bedside table for an evening snack.

5 quarts popped corn (2/3 cup popping corn kernels)
1/2 cup light corn syrup
2 cups light brown sugar
1 cup melted butter
1 teaspoon salt
1/2 teaspoon baking soda
1½ cups whole nuts (optional)

Preheat oven to 200°. Combine syrup, sugar, butter and salt in medium saucepan. Bring to boil; reduce heat to low and simmer 5 minutes. Remove from heat; add baking soda and stir with whisk until foamy. Pour over popped corn, stirring until evenly coated. Add nuts, if desired. Place corn in large baking dish. Bake 1 hour, stirring every 15 minutes. Remove from oven and spread on cookie sheets to cool. Store in airtight tins in cool place. Yield: About 5 quarts.

GATEWAY BED & BREAKFAST, MISSOURI

Florida Keys Hot Crab/Lobster Dip

3 ounces cream cheese
3 tablespoons mayonnaise
6 ounces crabmeat or lobster meat,
    picked over to remove cartilage
1 tablespoon lemon juice
1/4 teaspoon garlic salt

Preheat oven to 350°. In medium mixing bowl, blend cream cheese and mayonnaise until smooth. Stir in crabmeat or lobster, lemon juice and garlic salt. Combine well. Turn into greased, oven-proof casserole.* Bake for 30 minutes. Serve with crackers, chips or as a spread on Russian black bread. Yield: 4 servings.

*Make ahead to this point and refrigerate overnight.

Joan Hopp
BED & BREAKFAST OF THE KEYS, FLORIDA

■ As a mainstay, double recipe; serve over buttered pasta and sprinkle with toasted almond slivers. For your large gatherings, it triples nicely.

Friedrichsburg Kochkase

■ Wilhelmina is a gracious hostess who speaks fluent German and enjoys serving her guests in her lovely blumengarten, the result of constant personal love and tending. Her breakfasts are created usually after she meets her guests and has had a chance to learn their preferences.

This is one of her favorite menus. German Texan Special: Cranberry and apple juice combination (mainly because, in a crystal glass the color is delightful), sliced fresh fruit plate, hot local German cooked cheese on buttered pumpernickel bread, and thinly sliced venison sausage; followed by strawberry bread and freshly brewed coffee or herb tea.

"Friedrichsburg Kochkase" (cooked cheese) is the most loved delicacy throughout the German Hills of Texas. It is made by separating cow's milk, butter from cream, and putting the clabber into a cloth bag which is hung in the open to let the whey drip. Depending on the weather, when thoroughly dry, crumble the cheese into a bowl. Cover the bowl with a plate. In three or four days check the fermentation so that the cheese will melt when heated. Put in skillet over low heat. Add a bit of milk, salt to taste, let bubble and stir. Pour into bowl and serve. Each guest twists a knife and generously smears the cheese on buttered bread. ("Mit Musik" [or literally, to flavor it up] when cheese is put into skillet, sprinkle caraway seed or jalapeno peppers over it. This is a unique Mexican Texas contribution to an old German favorite.)

Wilhelmina's Host Home
THE BED & BREAKFAST SOCIETY, TEXAS

Judy's World-Famous Granola

Granola first appeared in the dietary doctrine of Dr. James Caleb Jackson, promoting temperance and healthful eating. This modern-day version is good dry, with milk as cereal or as a topping for fruits. Can be used also as an ingredient in cookies and muffins.

1/2 cup safflower oil
1/2 cup honey or corn syrup
1 teaspoon vanilla
5 cups rolled oats
1/2 cup shredded, unsweetened coconut
1/2 cup sunflower seeds
1/2 cup sesame seeds
1/4 cup wheat germ
1/2 cup chopped raw, unsalted nuts (walnut, almond or Brazil)
1/2 teaspoon salt

Preheat oven to 325°. In small saucepan, combine oil, honey or syrup and vanilla. Place dry ingredients in bowl large enough to allow for thorough mixing and toss to combine well. Pour hot mixture over dry ingredients, mixing well with wooden spoon. Spread thinly on baking sheet. Bake approximately 40 minutes, or until dry, stirring every 10 to 15 minutes to prevent burning. Cool and store in airtight container in cool, dry place. Keeps well. Yield: About 7 cups.

"One cup raisins or currants may be added to granola when removed from oven and still warm."

Judy Donaldson, Host
BED & BREAKFAST BIRMINGHAM, INC., ALABAMA

Marinated Chicken

"I suggest serving this in your favorite serving piece and surrounding with Melba rounds."

    2 chicken bouillon cubes
    Hot water
    3 chicken breasts, halved
    Salt
    4 garlic cloves, minced
    2 cups olive oil
    1 cup wine or tarragon vinegar
    2 bay leaves
    12 peppercorns
    5 to 6 medium onions, sliced
    2 cups sour cream

Dissolve bouillon in 1 cup hot water in 3-quart saucepan. Add chicken, salt to taste, garlic cloves and enough water to cover chicken. Simmer over medium heat until chicken is cooked. Drain, cool and remove chicken from bones; set aside.

In medium saucepan, combine oil, vinegar, 1/2 teaspoon salt, bay leaves, peppercorns and onions. Simmer 30 minutes over low heat. Fold in chicken until well coated. Chill in refrigerator several hours. When ready to serve, drain off and discard 1 cup of marinade; fold sour cream into chicken mixture. Yield: 12 to 14 servings for hors d'oeuvres or 6 to 8 for main course.

Shirley Jensen, Host
NEW ORLEANS BED & BREAKFAST, LOUISIANA

■ Heat slowly and try as an unusual "hot salad" entree, served over buttered spinach noodles. Garnish with cherry tomatoes and minced parsley.

Miracle Mushrooms

1 pound fresh mushrooms, washed and sliced
1 cup heavy cream
Freshly ground white pepper
1/2 teaspoon salt
Juice of 1/2 lemon

In large skillet, combine mushrooms, cream, pepper, salt and lemon juice. Simmer about 20 minutes over low heat, stirring occasionally. Spread on toast as a breakfast side dish with eggs. Serve immediately. Yield: About 2 cups.

"When thickened into a delectable spread, place in a ramekin and surround with Melba rounds, firm toast or crackers."

Wendy Berry, Host
THE B&B GROUP (NEW YORKERS
AT HOME) INC., NEW YORK

■ Fresh fettucine, covered with this stroganoff-type sauce, makes a great side dish.

Sausage Rolls

1 pound lean bulk sausage, the spicier the better
1/2 pound sharp Cheddar cheese, shredded
2 cups biscuit mix

In large mixing bowl, combine sausage, Cheddar and biscuit mix, mixing well. Mold mixture into 1½- or 2-inch rolls.* Preheat oven to 400°. Place sausage rolls, single layer, in baking dish or on a cookie sheet with edges. Bake approximately 10 minutes, turning once. Yield: Sixty 2-inch sausage rolls.

Terry suggests using a food processor for easier mixing of ingredients.

Terry Murray
BAY STREET INN, SOUTH CAROLINA

■ *Wrap around stuffed green olives, place on a cookie sheet in single layer and freeze. When frozen, wrap tightly in freezer bags. Bake for 15 to 20 minutes when needed. Serve with a coarsely-seeded mustard.

Stoddard Seafood Mousse

"We often serve this mousse to our guests, accompanied with a glass of wine, after 'show and tell' of our lovely house restoration.

"When I use a fish mold, I make scales of finely sliced cucumber, fins of carrots and eyes of olives with parsley eyelashes. Delicious served with crackers as an hors d'oeuvre or as a salad over greens."

    1 can (10½ ounces) tomato soup
    1 pound cream cheese
    2 packets unflavored gelatin
    1/2 cup cold water
    1 pound cooked shrimp, finely chopped, or whole baby shrimp
    1 cup mayonnaise, plus additional to grease mold
    1/3 cup chopped celery
    1/3 cup chopped green pepper
    1/3 cup minced onion

Bring soup to a boil in a 2-quart saucepan. Add cream cheese and whisk together until cheese melts and "sauce" is creamy. Dissolve gelatin in cold water, and stir into sauce. Remove from heat; set aside to cool, about 30 minutes. Stir in remaining ingredients. With additional mayonnaise, grease a 5½-cup mold. Pour mousse into mold, leaving 1/4-inch clearance from top. Cover with plastic wrap and refrigerate overnight.

To unmold, immerse mold in hot water, enough to reach top edges. When edges of mousse soften slightly, remove mold from water. Quickly flip over onto serving platter or place serving platter upside down onto top of mold. Holding platter and mold tightly, flip upright. Yield: 6 salad servings.

Barbara Hershey
"STODDARD-COOPER HOUSE"
BED & BREAKFAST SAVANNAH, GEORGIA

Tortillas Con Queso (Or Salsa)

As part of the Mexican influence on food so adaptable to the casual life style of Southern California, these finger foods can be found on patios or in front of TV's, with additional munchies nearby.

    Corn tortillas
    Oil for frying
    Shredded Cheddar or Jack cheese

Heat oil in skillet and fry tortillas until crisp. Drain on paper towel, then tear into small strips. Place shredded cheese on each strip and put in oven until cheese melts.
    Or, fry tortillas, drain, tear into strips and use as dippers for . . .

Salsa Dip

    2 fresh Anaheim (long, dark green) chili peppers
    2 ripe tomatoes
    1/2 small onion
    1 can (8 ounces) tomato sauce
    Salt to taste

Finely chop peppers, tomatoes and onions and mix together in a small bowl. Stir in tomato sauce and salt. May be made ahead and refrigerated. Remove 1 hour before serving and serve at room temperature.

J. Parker, Host
Eye Openers B&B Reservations, California

Index of Contributors

The Bed Post Writers Group would like to thank the gracious Bed and Breakfast hosts across the country who shared their recipes and "tricks of the trade" for making the thousands of guests who go through their homes feel welcome. These hosts enjoy sharing their lives, their homes and their recipes. Hospitality is their "trademark."

Whether you are a first-time B&B'er, or a veteran of many delightful Bed and Breakfast stays, you will see from the following list that you can travel across this great country and meet people in their own environments. What better way to travel?

You may contact any of the following contributors for brochures or information on Bed and Breakfast accommodations in their area.

ALABAMA
". . . safe, clean, comfortable accommodations in attractive homes with warm, intelligent people who balance friendliness with respect for privacy."
> Bed & Breakfast Birmingham, Inc.
> P.O. Box 31328, Birmingham, AL 35222
> Ruth Taylor (205) 591-6406

ALASKA
"Camai Cheechako . . . We welcome you to the Great Land with the 20-hour day that is not long enough to see it all!"
> Stay With A Friend (B&B Alaskan Style)
> Box 173-3605 Arctic Boulevard, Anchorage, AK 99503
> Irene Pettigrew (907) 274-6445

ARIZONA
". . . local color and local customs explained by friendly hosts who enjoy sharing their Western Hospitality."
> Bed and Breakfast in Arizona, Inc.
> 8433 North Black Canyon, Suite 160, Phoenix, AZ 85021
> Bessie Lipinski (602) 995-2831

ARKANSAS
> Ozark B&B (Booking British Guests)
> 1567 Porter Street, Batesville, AR 72501
> B. C. Jett (501) 793-4289

CALIFORNIA
"The hosts that offer accommodations in their homes are warm, congenial and love to entertain the out-of-town guests."
> American Family Inn, B&B San Francisco
> 2185-A Union Street, San Francisco, CA 94123
> Susan/Richard Kreibich (415) 931-3083

CALIFORNIA (Continued)

> B n' B Megan's Friends
> 2345 Cimarron Way, Los Osos, CA 93402
> Megan Backer (805) 528-6645

"Reservations arranged in comfortable private homes with complete breakfast."

> Bed & Breakfast International
> 151 Ardmore Road, Kensington, CA 94707
> Jean Brown (415) 525-4596

> Bed and Breakfast of Los Angeles
> 32127 Harborview Lane, Westlake Village, CA 91361
> Peg Marshall (213) 889-7325

"Rooms with mountain view—in a beautiful home—quiet area. Breakfast—homemade muffins—jams and jellies."

> Bed & Breakfast in Ojai
> 921 Patricia Court, Ojai, CA 93023
> Tiba G. Willner (805) 646-8337

> Bed and Breakfast—West Coast
> 4744 Third Street, Carpinteria, CA 93013
> Jim/Becky Wheeler (805) 684-3524

"The historic Dr. Briggs House, Sacramento's first Bed & Breakfast Inn offers a comfortable home-away-from-home atmosphere for business and pleasure travelers to the Capital City."

> The Briggs House
> 2209 Capitol Avenue, Sacramento, CA 95816
> Kathy Yates/Sue Garmston (916) 441-3214

". . . a mixture of lace, wicker, marble and quilting, with a collection of rag dolls and stuffed animals. . . A place where guests are transported to quieter times."

> Britt House
> 406 Maple Street, San Diego, CA 92103
> Daun Martin (714) 234-2926

"We want you to feel that every time you arrive at one of our houses, you are really coming home."

> California Bed and Breakfast Inn Service
> P.O. Box 1256, Chico, CA 95927
> Lynne Morgan (916) 343-9733

". . . strictly private homes that promise the comforts of home away from home."

> Carolyn's Bed & Breakfast Homes
> P.O. Box 84776, San Diego, CA 92138
> (619) 435-5009 / 481-7662

"As long-time residents of the Los Angeles/Pasadena area, we know the places and people to make your stay special."

> Eye Openers Bed & Breakfast Reservations
> P.O. Box 694, Altadena, CA 91001
> Ruth Judkins (213) 684-4428 / 797-2055

". . . there are NO SURPRISES when it comes to comfort and convenience, but you'll be constantly surprised by the way Gramma will pamper and spoil you."

> Gramma's Bed and Breakfast Inn
> 2740 Telegraph Avenue, Berkeley, CA 94705
> Suzanne/Dorothy Jackson (415) 549-2145

CALIFORNIA (Continued)

Home Suite Homes
1470 Firebird Way, Sunnyvale, CA 94087
Robert Rosen/Rhonda Robins (415) 733-7215

Homestay B&B
P.O. Box 326, Camberia, CA 93428
Alex Laputz (805) 927-4613

"Welcome to the special hospitality of Bed and Breakfast. You are invited to stay in an attractive home where you will be made to feel welcome . . . with hosts you will enjoy knowing, who will help you find the places and things you wish to do. It is an interesting and most friendly way to travel."
Rent-A-Room International
11531 Varna Street, Garden Grove, CA 92640
J. P. MacLachlan (714) 6381406

COLORADO

"Bed and Breakfast is an accommodation in a private home or small inn where the traveler is treated more like a guest than a source of income."
Bed & Breakfast Colorado
P.O. Box 20596, Denver, CO 80220
Rick Madden (303) 333-3340

". . . offers a unique atmosphere of lodging in the European tradition."
Bed & Breakfast Rocky Mountains
P.O. Box 804, Colorado Springs, CO 80901
Kate Peterson (303) 630-3433

CONNECTICUT

Nutmeg Bed & Breakfast
222 Girard Avenue, Hartford, CT 06105
Maxine Kates (203) 236-6698

DELAWARE

"The Sea-Vista Villa on Salt Pond is a small Bed & Breakfast guest house for adults only. The daily rate includes a full breakfast served on the terrace. Open May through Thanksgiving."
The Quiet Resort
Box 62, Bethany Beach, DE 19930
Dale M. Duvall (302) 539-3354
or
The Quiet Resorts
1346 Connecticut Avenue NW, Washington, DC 20036
Dale M. Duvall (202) 223-0322

DISTRICT OF COLUMBIA

Sweet Dreams & Toast, Inc.
P.O. Box 4835-0035, Washington, DC 20008
Eleanor K. Chastain (202) 483-9191

The Bed & Breakfast League, Ltd.
3639 Van Ness Street NW, Washington, DC 20008
Millie Croobey (202) 363-7767

FLORIDA

A&A Bed & Breakfast of Florida, Inc.
P.O. Box 1316, Winter Park, FL 32790
Bruni Fehner (305) 628-3233

Bed & Breakfast Co.
1205 Mariposa Avenue #233, Miami, FL 33146
Marcella Schaible (305) 661-3270

"Our hosts are people who have a sincere interest in providing guests with comfort, hospitality and their knowledge of the area."

Bed & Breakfast of the Florida Keys, Inc.
5 Man-O-War Drive, Marathon, FL 33050
Joan E. Hopp (305) 743-4118

Florida Suncoast Bed and Breakfast
P.O. Box 12, Palm Harbor, FL 33563
Carol J. Hart (813) 784-5118

"British style Bed & Breakfast in America. . ."

Sun & Fun Accommodations
3604 S.W. 23rd Street, Fort Lauderdale, FL 33312
Joanne Hewitson (305) 583-5157

Suncoast Accommodations
P.O. Box 8334, Madeira Beach, FL 33738
Bobbi Seligman (813) 360-1755

GEORGIA

"Staying overnight with local people has long been a tradition in Europe; we're lovers of Atlanta and want to introduce travelers to the gracious hospitality that made our city famous."

Bed & Breakfast Atlanta
1221 Fairview Road, NE, Atlanta, GA 30306
Paula Gris / Madalyne Eplan / Jane Carney (404) 378-6026

"Your hosts cordially invite you to stay in the garden level of their carefully restored historic home on beautiful Chippewa Square in the heart of Historic Savannah."

The Stoddard Cooper Inn
19 West Perry Street, Savannah, GA 31401
Barbara/David Hersey (912) 233-6809

HAWAII

"Bed & Breakfast brings the old world tradition of home sharing to Hawaii. Our hosts are warm, receptive people who wish to share their experience and love of the islands."

Bed & Breakfast Hawaii
Box 499 - Kapaa, Kapaa, HI 96746
Evie Warner (808) 822-1582

ILLINOIS

"Our hosts are pleasant, interesting individuals who are knowledgeable about their area and eager to offer Midwestern hospitality to enhance the quality of your visit to the Windy City."

Bed & Breakfast/Chicago, Inc.
1704 Crilly Court, Chicago, IL 60614
Mary Shaw (312) 951-0085

INDIANA
> Camel Lot
> 4512 West 131st Street, Westfield, IN 46074
> Moselle Schaffer (317) 873-4370

IOWA
> Bed & Breakfast in Iowa, Ltd.
> 7104 Franklin Avenue, Des Moines, IA 50322
> Iona Ansorge (515) 277-9018

"A quiet country inn for those who want a secluded place to retreat."
> Mason House Inn
> Bentonsport Iowa, c/o Keosauqua, IA 52565
> Burretta Redhead (319) 592-3133

KANSAS
"We love making new friends and exchanging ideas and ways of life, so we invite people to 'Come, Be One of Us' for awhile. . ."
> Bed 'n Breakfast on our Farm
> Route 1, Box 132, Wakefield, KS 67487
> Rod 'n Pearl Thurlow (913) 461-5596

> Kansas City Bed & Breakfast
> P.O. Box 14781, Lenexa, KS 66215
> Dale/Diane Kuhn (913) 268-4214

KENTUCKY
"Bed & Breakfast is for the sophisticated traveler adventurous enough to leave the well-worn path of impersonal, predictable hostelries."
> Kentucky Homes Bed & Breakfast
> 1431 St. James Court, Louisville, KY 40208
> Lillian Marshall / Jo DuBose Boone
> (502) 452-6629 / 635-7341

LOUISIANA
"Southern Hospitality in Private Homes . . . 'Linger longer, savor it all!'"
> New Orleans Bed & Breakfast
> P.O. Box 8163, New Orleans, LA 70182
> Sarah-Margaret Brown (504) 949-6705

"Offering you some of the best of Southern Hospitality and food. . ."
> Southern Comfort Bed & Breakfast Reservation Service
> 2856 Hundred Oaks, Baton Rouge, LA 70808
> Helen Heath (504) 346-1928 / 926-9784

MAINE
"The atmosphere in our 1850 farmhouse is friendly, informal and unhurried."
> Breezemere Farm
> Box 290, South Brooksville, ME 04617
> Joan Lippke (207) 326-8628

MAINE

"The atmosphere in our 1850 farmhouse is friendly, informal and unhurried."
Breezemere Farm
Box 290, South Brooksville, ME 04617
Joan Lippke (207) 326-8628

"B&B travel is a made-to-order pleasure for those who enjoy absorbing the true flavor of an area they visit, and who look forward to meeting local people along the way."
Bed & Breakfast Down East, Ltd.
Box 547, Eastbrook, ME 04634
Sally B. Godfrey (207) 565-3517

"Lodging in select private homes and small inns for discriminating guests who seek legendary Maine hospitality. . ."
Bed & Breakfast Registry of Maine
RFD 4, Box 4317, Brunswick, ME 04011
Ellie Welch/Peg Tierney (207) 781-4528

MARYLAND

"A registry of guest accommodations in host homes and yachts. . ."
Sharp-Adams, Inc.
8 Gentry Court, Annapolis, MD 21403
Cecily Sharp-Whitehill / B. J. Adams (301) 269-6232

MASSACHUSETTS

". . . a professional reservation service offering travelers comfortable lodging and breakfast in the warmth of private homes."
Bed & Breakfast Associates Bay Colony, Ltd.
P.O. Box 166, Babson Park Branch, Boston, MA 02157
Phyllis Levenson / Arline Kardasis / Marilyn Mitchell (617) 872-6990

"Colonial Hospitality with a Continental Flair"
Berkshire/Pioneer Valley Bed & Breakfast
141 Newton Road, Springfield, MA 01118
Tim/Mary Allen (413) 783-5111

"All seasons—all New England accommodations in private homes and small inns."
Pineapple Hospitality, Inc.
384 Rodney French Boulevard, New Bedford, MA 02744
Joan Brownhill (617) 997-9952

MICHIGAN

Betsy Ross Bed & Breakfast
3057 Betsy Ross Drive, Bloomfield Hills, MI 48013
Norma Buzan (313) 646-5357

Wellman Accommodations
205 Main Street, Horton, MI 49246
Karen D. Gauntlett (517) 563-2231

MINNESOTA

Bed & Breakfast Upper Midwest
P.O. Box 28036, Minneapolis, MN 55428
Maryann J. Kudalis (612) 535-7135

Evelos Bed and Breakfast
2301 Bryant Avenue South, Minneapolis, MN 55405
(612) 374-9656

MISSISSIPPI

"Anchuca (Indian for Happy Home) will pamper you with luxurious surroundings, Southern-style breakfast and lots of Southern hospitality."
"Anchuca"
1010 First East, Vicksburg, MS 39108
Kathy McKay (601) 636-4931

MISSOURI

Gateway Bed & Breakfast
16 Green Acres, St. Louis, MO 63137
Evelyn Ressler (314) 868-2335

Mid-Missouri Bed and Breakfast Service
Route 70, Box 833, Camdenton, MO 65020
Barbara Fredholm/Gladys Morgan (314) 346-3944

Ozark Mountain Country Bed & Breakfast Service
Box 295, Branson, MO 65616
Kay Cameron (417) 334-4720

MONTANA

Frontier Executive Retreats, Inc.
P.O. Box 322, Kalispell, MT 59901
Sylva B. Jones (406) 257-4476

NEBRASKA

". . . offers tourists a personalized visit to the state."
Nebraska Bed & Breakfast
1464 28th Avenue NE, Columbus, NE 68601
Marlene Van Lent (402) 564-7591

NEW HAMPSHIRE

"Fine European cuisine and comfortable lodging in the old world tradition."
The Bernerhof
P.O. Box 381, Route 302, Glen, New Hampshire 03838
Ted Wroblewski (603) 383-4414

Cheney House
40 Highland Street, P.O. Box 683, Ashland, NH 03217
Daryl F. Mooney

"Whatever the season, we offer good food, comfortable lodging and a casual atmosphere."
Loch Lyme Lodge
Lyme, NH 03768
Judy/Paul Barker (603) 795-2141

"Affordable first class country comfort and quaintness unequaled."
Whitneys' Village Inn
Route 16B, Jackson, NH 03846
Darrell Trapp (603) 383-6886

NEW JERSEY

"From the beginning of your day with our 'community' breakfast, through our late afternoon get-togethers on the veranda, you always feel that special blend of intimate atmosphere and Victorian elegance when you are a guest at . . .

The Abbey
Columbia Avenue and Gurney Street, Cape May, NJ 08204
Jay/Marianne Schatz (609) 884-4506

"At our Victorian Bed and Breakfast Guest House, we comfort and delight you . . . all sumptuous, gourmet and lovingly created for you."

Barnard-Good House at Cape May
238 Perry Street, Cape May, NJ 08204
Nan/Tom Hawkins (609) 884-5381

"Share the warm conversation and friendliness that's kindled at our table ... strangers are no more, ages and occupations aren't significant; there's a real communication among people, just relaxing, just being people."

Mainstay Inn
635 Columbia Avenue, Cape May, NJ 08204
Tom/Sue Carroll (609) 884-8690

NEW MEXICO

"Eat, rest, explore at 'The Little House' . . .

La Casita
R.R. 10, Box 137, Glenwood, NM 88039
Dan/Sally Campbell (505) 539-2124

NEW YORK

A Reasonable Alternative, Inc.
Bed & Breakfast on Long Island
117 Spring Street, Suite C, Port Jefferson, NY 11777
Kathleen Dexter (516) 928-4034 / 473-7402

Bed & Breakfast of Central New York
1846 Bellevue Avenue, Syracuse, NY 13204
Linda Rackard / Mary Lou Karrat (315) 472-5050

The B&B Group (New Yorkers at Home) Inc.
301 East 60th Street, New York, NY 10022
Farla Zammit (212) 838-7015

Urban Ventures
P.O. Box 426, New York, NY 10024
Mary McAulay / Fran Tesser (212) 594-5650

NORTH CAROLINA

"The Flint Street Inn offers three bedrooms with two shared baths in the European tradition of Bed and Breakfast."

Flint Street Inn
116 Flint Street, Asheville, NC 28801
Rick/Lynne Vogel (704) 253-6723

OHIO

"BB&B is a group of host homes throughout Ohio ready to welcome you to a most pleasant way to enjoy a home away from home in the fullest sense."
Buckeye Bed & Breakfast
P.O. Box 130, Powell, OH 43065
Don/Sally Hollenback (614) 548-4555

Columbus Bed & Breakfast (German Village)
763 South 3rd Street, Columbus, OH 43206
Fred Holdridge/Howard Burns
(614) 443-3680 / 444-8888

OKLAHOMA

Bed & Breakfast Oklahoma
P.O. Box 32045, Oklahoma City, OK 73123
Jo Ann Hamilton (405) 946-2894

OREGON

Northwest Bed & Breakfast, Inc.
7707 S.W. Locust Street, Portland, OR 97223
Laine Friedman (503) 246-8366

"Indulge yourself in an atmosphere that blends grace with casualness."
The Coach House Inn
Seventy Coolidge Street, Ashland, OR 97520
Jack/Pamela Evans (503) 482-2257

PENNSYLVANIA

"Based on the European concept, this comfortable, inexpensive and individual way to travel grows increasingly popular."
Bed & Breakfast of Philadelphia
P.O. Box 680, Devon, PA 19333-0680
Joanne Goins / Sandra Fullerton / Carol Yarrow (215) 688-1753 Telex 902320

Bed & Breakfast of the Southeast Pennsylvania
Box 278, R.D. #1, Barto, PA 19504
Joyce Stevenson (215) 845-3526

Bed & Breakfast of the Poconos, NE
P.O. Box 115, Bear Creek, PA 18602
Ann Magagna (717) 472-3145

"In selected private homes, the hospitality of our city shines through."
Pittsburgh Bed & Breakfast
P.O. Box 25353, Pittsburgh, PA 15242
Karen Krull (412) 241-5746

"Our hosts are chosen for their friendly personalities and charming homes. Often their individual tastes and lifestyles will reflect those of your own."
Rest & Repast Bed & Breakfast Service
Pine Grove Mills, PA 16868
Linda C. Feltman / Brent R. Peters (814) 238-1484

RHODE ISLAND
"We welcome all our past and future friends to come and enjoy the comfortable atmosphere of. . .
The Brinley Victorian
23 Brinley Street, Newport, RI 02840
Susan Jenkins (401) 849-7645

Castle Keep Bed & Breakfast Registry
44 Everett Street, Newport, RI 02840
Audrey Grimes / Dorothy Ranhofer (401) 846-0362

SOUTH CAROLINA
"Guest accommodations in the Lewis Reeves Sams House of 1852, a restored ante-bellum home . . ."
Bay Street Inn
601 Bay Street, Beaufort, SC 29902
Terry/David Murray (803) 524-7720

Historic Charleston Bed & Breakfast
23 Wentworth Street, Charleston, SC 29401
Charlotte Fairey (803) 722-6606

SOUTH DAKOTA
"A stranger is a friend you have yet to meet . . ."
The Alden Skoglunds
"Skoglund Farm"
Canova, SD 57321
Delores Skoglund (605) 247-3445

TENNESSEE
"Southern hospitality is alive and well."
Nashville Bed & Breakfast
1101 17th Avenue South, Box 15651, Nashville, TN 37215
Betty Cordellos (615) 327-4546

TEXAS
". . . to enhance fellowship and friendship throughout the world . . ."
The Bed & Breakfast Society
330 West Main Street, Fredericksburg, TX 78624
Kenn Knopp (512) 997-4712

"Welcome to an enriching blend of cultures, customs, food and hosts who are genuinely interested in sharing their Texas-style hospitality and knowledge of the local area with you."
Bed & Breakfast Texas Style
4224 West Red Bird Lane, Dallas, TX 75237
Ruth Wilson (214) 298-5433 / 8586

UTAH
Bed'n Breakfast Association of Utah
P.O. Box 16465, Salt Lake City, UT 84116
Barbara Baker / Nadine Smith (801) 532-7076 / 486-6339

VERMONT

"American B&B offers the traveler a most unique way to enjoy Vermont. Most of our host homes are dairy farms or country homes located far from any commercial sleeping establishment. Guests can experience how special the country is when they get off the most traveled roads and venture onto the byways.;;

American Bed & Breakfast
Box 983, St. Albans, VT 05478
Bob/Linda Precoda (802) 524-4731

VIRGINIA

"Whether you plan to be in Richmond on business or for pleasure, let us arrange a reservation that will afford you a unique, more personalized style of hospitality."

Bensonhouse of Richmond
P.O. Box 15131, Richmond, VA 23227
Lyn M. Benson (804) 321-6277 / 649-4601

Guesthouses Reservation Service
P.O. Box 5737, Charlottesville, VA 22903
Sally Reger (804) 979-7264 / 979-8327

WASHINGTON

"Reasonable private home accommodations."

Pacific Bed & Breakfast
701 NW 60th Street, Seattle, WA 98107
Irmgard Castleberry (206) 784-0539

WEST VIRGINIA

"Old-fashioned hospitality welcomes the crowd-weary traveler."

Countryside Bed & Breakfast
Box 57, Summit Point, WV 25446
Lisa/Daniel Hileman 725-2614

WISCONSIN

"... offers you local color and relaxing vacations in private homes with friendly hosts. Each accommodation is carefully selected for hospitality, cleanliness and comfort, A variety of extras is offered for that personal touch."

Bed & Breakfast Guest-Homes
Route #2, Algoma, WI 54201
Eilene Wood (414) 743-9742

WYOMING

Bunkhouse
P.O. Box 384, Moose, WY 83012
(307) 383-2015

Alphabetical List of Recipes

Recipe Index

East Woods Press Books

American Bed & Breakfast
  Cook Book, The
America's Grand Resort Hotels
Backcountry Cooking
Berkshire Trails for Walking & Ski Touring
Best Bed & Breakfast in the World, The
Blue Ridge Mountain Pleasures
California Bed & Breakfast
Campfire Chillers
Campfire Songs
Canoeing the Jersey Pine Barrens
Carolina Curiosities
Carolina Seashells
Carpentry: Some Tricks of the Trade from
  an Old-Style Carpenter
Catfish Cookbook, The
Charlotte: A Touch of Gold
Complete Guide to Backpacking
  in Canada
Creative Gift Wrapping
Day Trips From Baltimore
Day Trips From Cincinnati
Day Trips From Houston
Drafting: Tips and Tricks on Drawing and
  Designing House Plans
Exploring Nova Scotia
Fifty Years on the Fifty:
  The Orange Bowl Story
Fructose Cookbook, The
Grand Old Ladies
Grand Strand: An Uncommon Guide
  to Myrtle Beach, The
Healthy Trail Food Book, The
Hiking from Inn to Inn
Hiking Virginia's National Forests
Historic Country House Hotels
Hosteling USA, Third Edition
How to Afford Your Own Log Home
How to Play With Your Baby
Indiana: Off the Beaten Path
Interior Finish: More Tricks of the Trade
Just Folks: Visitin' with Carolina People
Kays Gary, Columnist
Maine Coast: A Nature Lover's
  Guide, The
Making Food Beautiful
Mid-Atlantic Guest House Book, The
New England Guest House Book, The
New England: Off the Beaten Path
Ohio: Off the Beaten Path
Parent Power!
Parks of the Pacific Coast
Race, Rock and Religion
River Reflections
Rocky Mountain National Park Hiking Trails
Saturday Notebook, The
Sea Islands of the South

Separation and Divorce in North Carolina
South Carolina Hiking Trails
Southern Guest House Book, The
Southern Rock: A Climber's Guide
  to the South
Sweets Without Guilt
Tar Heel Sights: Guide to North Carolina's
  Heritage
Tennessee Trails
Toys That Teach Your Child
Train Trips: Exploring America by Rail
Trout Fishing the Southern Appalachians
Vacationer's Guide to Orlando and
  Central Florida, A
Walks in the Catskills
Walks in the Great Smokies
Walks with Nature in Rocky Mountain
  National Park
Whitewater Rafting in Eastern America
Wildflower Folklore
Woman's Journey, A
You Can't Live on Radishes

Order from:

The East Woods Press
429 East Boulevard
Charlotte, NC 28203